DATE DUE

DEMCO 38-296

GREAT WRITERS OF THE ENGLISH LANGUAGE

British Women Novelists

TAFF CREDITS

Executive Editor
Reg Wright

Series Editor
Sue Lyon

Editors
Jude Welton
Sylvia Goulding

Deputy Editors
Alice Peebles
Theresa Donaghey

Features Editors
Geraldine McCaughrean
Emma Foa
Ian Chilvers

Art Editors
Kate Sprawson
Jonathan Alden
Helen James

Designers
Simon Wilder
Frank Landamore

Senior Picture Researchers
Julia Hanson
Vanessa Fletcher
Georgina Barker

Picture Clerk
Vanessa Cawley

Production Controllers
Judy Binning
Tom Helsby

Editorial Secretaries
Fiona Bowser
Sylvia Osborne

Managing Editor
Alan Ross

Editorial Consultant
Maggi McCormick

Publishing Manager
Robert Paulley

Reference Edition Published 1989
Published by Marshall Cavendish Corporation
147 West Merrick Road
Freeport, Long Island
N.Y. 11520

Typeset by Litho Link Ltd., Welshpool
Printed and Bound in Italy by
L.E.G.O. S.p.a. Vicenza

LIBRARY OF CONGRESS
Library of Congress Cataloging-in-Publication Data
Great Writers of the English Language
     p. cm.
     Includes index vol.
     ISBN 1-85435-000-5 (set): $399.95
     1. English literature — History and criticism. 2. English
literature — Stories, plots, etc. 3. American literature — History
and criticism. 4. American literature — Stories, plots, etc.
5. Authors. English — Biography. 6. Authors. American — Biography.
I. Marshall Cavendish Corporation.
PR85.G66 1989
820'.9 – dc19   88-21077
                                                             CIP

ISBN 1–85435–000–5 (set)
ISBN 1–85435–004–8 (vol)

GREAT WRITERS OF THE ENGLISH LANGUAGE

British Women Novelists

Charlotte Brontë

Emily Brontë

Elizabeth Gaskell

George Eliot

MARSHALL CAVENDISH · NEW YORK · TORONTO · LONDON · SYDNEY

CONTENTS

CHARLOTTE BRONTË

✦ *1816-1855* ✦

Sole surviving sister of a tragic and talented family, Charlotte Brontë
was the only one to receive public acclaim before she, too, died
prematurely. In early adulthood she shared the precarious lot of
Victorian women, forced to live a 'walking nightmare of poverty
and self-suppression'. Only literary success gained her some
independence, ironically achieved by adopting a sexless pseudonym.
Only now is she recognized as a truly revolutionary writer, exploring
her themes with startling passion and clarity.

A Passionate Individual

**Living in a remote Yorkshire parsonage, Charlotte Brontë's few
real experiences were blighted by family deaths, social stigma
and unrequited love. But she found an escape through fantasy.**

Like Jane Eyre, Charlotte Brontë was a small,
plain woman, who was fiercely independent,
passionate in spirit and had little interest in the
conventional life to which Victorian women were expected to aspire. Yet her life was a sacrifice to duty –
despite her yearning for greater things, she played out
the roles of dutiful daughter and accommodating wife.

She was born on 21 April 1816 at Thornton vicarage
in Yorkshire, the third daughter of Patrick Brontë, the
Irish curate of the parish, and his gentle, Cornish wife
Maria. Around the time of Charlotte's fourth birthday,
her father was appointed perpetual curate of nearby
Haworth, and the family made the ten-mile journey
there in a wagon and seven carts. By now, three more
children had been born – Branwell, Emily and Anne.

The austere parsonage which became their lifelong
home, the steep hill-village with its dark cobbled
streets, and the bleak beauty of the surrounding moors
were formative influences on the children.

MOTHERLESS CHILDREN

The year after the family's arrival at Haworth, Maria
Brontë died of cancer. Her sister, Elizabeth Branwell,
was persuaded to leave sunny Penzance to look after
the six motherless children in damp, windy Yorkshire.
Though conscientious in her duties, 'Aunt' showed
little affection for her charges, and even less for the
wild countryside they so loved.

In 1824, Patrick Brontë managed to find a school
for the four older girls. For only £14 a year, the Rev.
Carus Wilson would board and educate the daughters
of the clergy at Cowan Bridge. But unknown to Mr
Brontë, the size of the fee reflected the neglect and
undernourishment suffered by the girls.

A wealthy evangelical clergyman, the Rev. Wilson

The family home
*The Brontë family – the
Reverend, his wife and their
six children – moved to
Haworth parsonage when
Charlotte was four, and it
remained their lifelong
home. Papa Brontë outlived
all his children and died there.*

Mother and aunt
*Charlotte's warm-hearted
mother Maria (inset, far
right) died the year after the
family's arrival at Haworth.
Her place was taken by her
austere sister, 'Aunt
Branwell' (inset, right).*

The Brontë Society/Mansell Collection

The Brontë Society

Key Dates

1816 born at Thornton

1820 family moves to Haworth parsonage

1824–5 pupil at Cowan Bridge; two sisters die

1831 goes to Roe Head

1835–8 teacher at Roe Head

1839 first post as a governess

1842 pupil at Pensionnat Heger, Brussels. Falls in love with M. Heger

1843–4 teacher at the Pensionnat

1847 *Jane Eyre* published

1848–49 Branwell, Emily and Anne die

1854 marries Rev Arthur Bell Nicholls

1855 dies at Haworth

aimed to prepare the daughters of poorer clergymen for a life of self-denial and submission by breaking their spirit with severe frugality, continuous punishment and repression. Such treatment had the opposite effect on the eight-year-old Charlotte: it instilled in her a deep, bitter and lasting resentment which she expressed some 20 years later in *Jane Eyre*.

In the novel, Carus Wilson becomes the harsh "black marble clergyman" Mr Brocklehurst, and Cowan Bridge becomes the hateful institution Lowood, Charlotte's gentle, submissive (and untidy) eldest sister Maria becomes the fictional Helen Burns. Like Helen, Maria died of consumption (tuberculosis), which she contracted at school. A month later, in June 1825, the second sister, Elizabeth, died of the same illness. Charlotte and Emily were brought home.

For the next six years, Charlotte settled into the enclosed life of the parsonage. The remaining children were left very much to their own devices: 'Aunt' kept a certain distance from them, and 'Papa' was a still remoter figure behind his study walls, and took his meals alone. So the young Brontës drew closer together and soon became immersed in telling, then writing stories about fantasy worlds they created.

IMAGINARY GLASS TOWN

The story-telling began in 1826, when Papa brought home a box of wooden soldiers. All four children had a soldier, each with its own imaginary kingdom, which together formed the 'Great Glass Town Confederacy'. Soon Charlotte and Branwell introduced an imaginary counterpart of their great hero the Duke of Wellington into the fantasies, then invented a special kingdom called Angria for his imaginary son Arthur Wellesley. In Charlotte's romantic fantasies about Arthur, he becomes the charismatic Duke of Zamorna, with two wives and several mistresses.

In 1830, Mr Brontë suffered a serious illness. It brought home to him the fact that – lacking any conventional training – his children would become paupers if he died. So, with financial help from her godparents, Charlotte was sent to school again – to Miss Wooler's establishment in an elegant country house at Roe Head.

Mary Taylor, who was to become her lifelong friend, records her arrival one cold January morning in 1831: 'in very old-fashioned clothes, and looking very cold and miserable . . . She looked like a little old woman, so short sighted that she always appeared

Deaths at school
Charlotte and three of her sisters were sent to Cowan Bridge in 1824. Only two survived.

A friend for life
(below) Charlotte met Ellen Nussey at Roe Head school, and they became faithful friends.

The Brontë Society

to be seeking something, and moving her head from side to side to catch a sight of it. She was very shy and nervous, and spoke with a strong Irish accent'. When invited to join in game-playing, 'she said that she had never played and could not play'.

Despite Charlotte's shyness, her sharp intellect soon took her to the top of the school, and she made a second lifelong friend – Ellen Nussey. Within 18 months, having absorbed all Roe Head had to teach, she returned home to Haworth.

The Writer's Life

The next three years were spent in domestic quietude, or absorbed in writing romantic Angrian dramas. Then, when Charlotte was 19, Miss Wooler offered her a post as assistant teacher at Roe Head, with a tiny salary and free schooling for one of her sisters. Despite her limited experience of normal childhood, the opportunity to help the family was too good to miss.

Charlotte felt oppressed – understandably – by the enforced sociability of school life: 'Stupidity the atmosphere, school-books the employment, asses the society', she noted bitterly in her journal. After almost three years of depression, her health failed and she returned to the quiet intensity of the family home.

Her next venture into the world was equally unhappy. In May 1839 – two months after turning down a proposal from Ellen's brother, the Rev. Henry Nussey – Charlotte became a temporary governess to the Sidgwicks of Stonegappe near Skipton. She left in July. The little Sidgwicks were 'devils incarnate' – 'more riotous, perverse, unmanageable cubs never grew'.

A month after her return, she received and rejected another proposal – this time from an impetuous young Irish curate who had been captivated by her during a single visit to her father.

Two years passed at Haworth before Charlotte found another position, again as a governess – this time with the Whites of Rawdon, Leeds. The Whites were more agreeable than the Sidgwicks, but Charlotte was peculiarly ill-equipped for such employment. To the already difficult lot of a governess she brought a shyness, a social awkwardness and a proud consciousness of her personal superiority.

ADVENTURE IN BELGIUM

Charlotte finally hit upon a plan that seemed to offer a decent future for herself and her sisters – they would open their own school. Amazingly, the obstacles were overcome. 'Aunt Branwell' was persuaded that a school would be a good investment for her capital, and even agreed to finance the necessary preliminary: a course of study that would give the girls a proper command of French and German. In 1842, a French school in Brussels, the Pensionnat Heger, accepted Charlotte and Emily's application.

The Pensionnat Heger was a spacious and well-run school for girls, presided over by Madame Claire Heger. Charlotte worked there with her accustomed zeal, and made rapid progress, although she and Emily had little or nothing to do with their fellow pupils. Charlotte found them 'singularly cold, selfish, animal and inferior', making no allowance for the fact that they were just schoolgirls. Their easy-going Roman Catholicism outraged her puritanical notions.

One Catholic was excepted from these strictures. Monsieur Constantin Heger spent most of his time teaching at a neighbouring boys' school, but he lived at his wife's establishment and gave some lessons there. A volatile, black-moustachioed figure in his early thirties, Heger was a passionate, exacting teacher who often reduced Charlotte to tears; whereupon 'Monsieur' became contrite and proffered handkerchieves and bonbons to repair the damage. Perhaps Heger, her 'Black Swan', reminded Charlotte of her dark Angrian heroes. In any event, she fell in love with him.

National Portrait Gallery

The Brontë Society

In November 1842, following the death of 'Aunt Branwell', Charlotte and Emily returned to Haworth. Charlotte soon went back to Brussels as a teacher. Without Emily she was isolated: 'I get on here from day to day in a Robinson-Crusoe-like sort of way; very lonely, but that does not signify', and was still at odds with her Catholic colleagues and pupils. But she had the joy of giving lessons to Monsieur who had decided to learn English.

Inevitably, Madame noticed the little English-woman's adoration of her husband and, without the slightest fuss, took measures to reduce their contact to a minimum. Soon Charlotte felt spied on, although it is impossible to say how much of this was in her own guilty imagination. In January 1844, after a year as a teacher, she left the Pensionnat with a diploma, the warm good wishes of Monsieur and Madame, and an intense unrequited passion.

Returning to Haworth from her Belgian adventures, Charlotte found her father near-blinded by cataracts,

and realized that it would be impossible to leave him: her plans for a school would come to nothing. In her loneliness, she wrote Monsieur letters that, while falling just short of an open declaration of devotion, were embarrassingly ardent.

DESPERATE LETTERS

As she waited in vain for a letter from Monsieur, her desperation increased. In November 1845, nearly two years after she had seen him, she wrote: 'To forbid me to write to you, to refuse to answer me, would be to tear from me my only joy on earth . . . when day by day I await a letter, and when day by day disappointment comes . . . I lose appetite and sleep – I pine away.'

Charlotte had renounced Angria in 1839, and had written little since. But her misery over Heger prompted her to compose a good deal of verse. Then, in the autumn of 1845, she discovered some of Emily's poems and realized their exceptional quality. This

Cloistered creativity
After the deaths of their eldest sisters, the four remaining Brontë children spent their childhood and early teenage years at Haworth in virtual isolation from the outside world – with little contact even with the adults of the family. 'Aunt Branwell' spent much of her time in her room, while Papa shut himself up in the study, leaving the children to amuse then.selves in the parlour (left). With no outsiders to play with, the young Brontës turned to each other for stimulation and created an imaginary world together. Later, it was during evenings in the parlour that Charlotte, Emily and Anne (shown above, right to left, in a painting by Branwell) wrote the novels which finally won for them the attentions of the literary world.

THE FAMILY FAILURE

Patrick Branwell Brontë was a year younger than Charlotte, and her chief collaborator in their mighty childhood epics. As the only son, the hopes of the family fell on him, but he was never able to escape the fantasy world of childhood.

Branwell boasted about his talents, but drank them away at the Black Bull, failing miserably to make anything of his early artistic ability, and not even managing to hold down a job as a railway clerk. In 1843, he was taken on as a tutor, but was sacked two years later. He declared that this was because of his passionate relationship with the mistress of the house.

Returning to Haworth, Branwell's drinking increased and he became addicted to opium, begging it from the druggist while the rest of the family was at church. 'He thought of nothing but stunning or drowning his agony of mind', Charlotte wrote, 'No one in the house could have rest'. Branwell's alternating stupor and delirium ended in 1848, when he died suddenly of consumption.

The Brontë Society

The Brontë Society

The only brother
(left) In this teenage portrait of himself and his sisters Branwell shows himself in an upright, 'manly' pose with his gun. But the realistic demands of manhood proved too much for him to cope with. While his sisters escaped their narrow lot through writing, Branwell found his escape in delirium induced by drugs and alcohol.

Fantasy lands
(above) It is thought that Charlotte painted this water-colour of the imaginary 'Bay of Glass Town'. For six years, she and Branwell worked together on the Glass Town sagas that they based in the fictional kingdom of 'Angria': Charlotte wrote the tales of romance, and Branwell created charismatic, warring heroes that he could never live up to.

seems to have awakened her powers of leadership. Though she had no illusions about her own poetic talent, she mobilized her sisters, and the three women put together a volume of poems. Charlotte found a publisher of religious books who was willing to produce it – at the authors' expense.

CURRER, ELLIS AND ACTON BELL

When the slim volume appeared, the authors were named as Currer (Charlotte), Ellis (Emily) and Acton (Anne) Bell. The pseudonyms were chosen because they were sexually ambiguous, leaving it open to question whether the versifiers were male or female; 'Bell' was taken, as a joke, from the middle name of the Rev. Brontë's new curate, Arthur Bell Nicholls.

Poems was not a success – only two copies were sold – but all three sisters were now writing hard. Charlotte finished *The Professor*; Emily's *Wuthering Heights* and Anne's *Agnes Grey* were written at about the same time. For several months Charlotte patiently sent them off, only to receive them back, rejected.

In July 1847 she eventually found a publisher for her sisters, but not for *The Professor*. The publishing firm of Smith, Elder also returned her novel, but intimated that a three-volume novel by Currer Bell would merit their careful attention. Charlotte sent off *Jane Eyre* which she had recently completed, and the miracle occurred: it was accepted and published within six weeks. And its reception was rapturous.

'Currer Bell' was famous, and his/her sex and identity were the subjects of wide speculation. The publisher of Emily's and Anne's books, T.C. Newby even attempted to cash in by implying that they might be Currer Bell's works. When he stated that Anne's

Curate's daughter
Charlotte's father (above), the Rev. Patrick Brontë was a constant but remote figure in her life. Born an Irish peasant, he climbed the social scale to become a Cambridge graduate and changed his name from Brunty to Brontë before settling into the curacy at Haworth. He outlived his wife and all his children.

Curate's wife
The Rev. Arthur Bell Nicholls (right) was curate to Charlotte's father for five years before he plucked up enough courage to ask for her hand. She was initially unimpressed, but his passion persuaded her.

Passion rejected
When Charlotte was 26, she and Emily travelled to Belgium to complete their education at the Pensionnat Heger in Brussels (right). Charlotte was impressed by the beauty of the city, but an even stronger impression was made by her teacher Monsieur Heger (below). Charlotte became desperately infatuated with her 'master', but he was married, and showed no sign of returning her love. This unrequited passion found expression in her last novel Villette.

Tenant of Wildfell Hall was by 'Currer', Charlotte and Anne decided to prove their separate existences.

They walked through a thunderstorm to Keighley, caught trains to Leeds and London, and presented themselves to George Smith of Smith, Elder. When Charlotte showed him one of the firm's letters addressed to Currer Bell Esq., he said sharply, 'Where did you get this?'. But he was soon convinced that the two little ladies in quaint old-fashioned dresses were indeed Currer and Acton Bell, and gallantly escorted them to the opera that evening.

Meanwhile, Branwell had proved unable to apply himself to any one thing, and had begun a rapid decline – wandering around in a drunken stupor, begging money from the sexton to buy more alcohol. Charlotte had little sympathy for her brother's weaknesses: 'he will never be fit for much', she told Ellen Nussey.

FAMILY DEATHS

On 24 September 1848, Branwell died of consumption. Emily and Anne caught the disease and were carried off within a few months. By spring 1849, Charlotte had lost all her family except Papa. She was condemned to a strange dual existence: for most of the year she lived in the lonely parsonage, the sole prop of a father who nonetheless continued to take his meals apart from her. But the solitude was broken by forays into the great world, where her reputation won her invitations to meet famous people. One such acquaintance, who became a close friend, was the novelist Elizabeth (Mrs) Gaskell – her *Life of Charlotte Brontë* is the definitive biography.

It seems likely that she hoped for a proposal from her publisher George Smith, but he never advanced beyond effusive friendship. Another member of his firm, James Taylor, did court her. Although she wavered, she could not overcome a fundamental physical revulsion: when he came near her, her 'veins ran ice'.

In December 1852, shortly after finishing *Villette*, the novel in which she evoked – and perhaps exorcised – the spell of Monsieur Heger, Charlotte received another offer of marriage from an unexpected quarter. The stammered proposal came from her father's curate of five years' standing, Arthur Bell Nicholls. Charlotte considered Nicholls a narrow-minded, boring high-churchman, nothing like her intellectual equal. But his scarcely bridled passion affected her.

Her father vehemently opposed the match. Nicholls responded dramatically – he broke down during a Communion service, refused to eat and drink, and volunteered to be a missionary in Australia (but took another curacy in Yorkshire). He wrote to Charlotte again and again – and eventually she secretly replied. In 1854 she promised to become his wife.

Charlotte and Arthur were married on 29 June 1854. Patrick Brontë refused to attend, and her old headmistress, Miss Wooler, gave her away. Ellen Nussey was the only guest. The couple spent their honeymoon in Arthur's native Ireland, then returned to Haworth where Charlotte settled into parish activity – 'my time is not my own now'.

She was soon pregnant, but morning sickness, endless nausea and vomiting proved too much for her frail body. On her deathbed she said to Arthur, 'I am not going to die, am I? He will not separate us — we have been so happy'. But she did die, on the night of 31 March 1855, leaving her husband, 'sitting desolate and alone in the old grey house'.

Fact or Fiction

THE MAD WOMAN IN THE ATTIC

The chilling image of mad Mrs Rochester locked in the attic of Thornfield Hall seems too horrific to be anything but the creation of Charlotte Brontë's imagination – yet it had a factual basis. When Charlotte was a governess, she visited Norton Conyers Hall near Ripon. The old house still stands today – an atmospheric place, strongly echoing Thornfield, and, tellingly, associated with an 18th-century legend of a madwoman locked away upstairs. Moreover, in 1845, Charlotte went to North Lees Hall near Sheffield, an old farm belonging to a family called *Eyre*. Here too there was a legend of a madwoman (this one perished in a fire). In an age when good asylums were few and far between, many caring families chose to keep their mad relatives at home.

Closeted madwoman
When his attempts to marry Jane Eyre bigamously are foiled, Rochester is forced to reveal his lunatic wife – whom he has kept locked in the attic. Charlotte may have drawn her inspiration for this savage figure from the legend of Norton Conyers Hall (left).

Simon Warner

Dulac/J. M. Dent/Mary Evans Picture Library

JANE EYRE

Charlotte Brontë's first and finest romantic novel explores a Victorian dilemma – an intelligent young woman's right to love and be loved, and yet retain her independent spirit.

E. M. Osborn: Home Thoughts (Detail)/Fine Art Photographic Library

Jane Eyre is remarkable for being both a powerful and atmospheric romantic novel, and a highly original account of an unloved orphan girl's development into an independent woman. Charlotte Brontë drew many of her characters from people she knew and she presents them with a startling psychological realism that was, for her time, revolutionary. Another of her gifts was for creating a kind of prose that is often quite poetic in its beauty, and matches the novel's passionate intensity.

Charlotte Brontë's tale bears the stamp of direct experience, and she tells it with honesty and candour. Her determination to uphold the right of an ordinary girl to love and be loved on her own terms and on equal terms, scandalized a few, but earned her the admiration – and probably the gratitude – of many of her readers.

GUIDE TO THE PLOT

The story opens in winter in Gateshead Hall, where Jane, a penniless ten-year-old orphan, lives with her Aunt Reed, and cousins John, Eliza and Georgiana. Jane is spurned by her Aunt, and bullied and scorned by her cousins. Her sufferings reach a peak, when, for a punishment, she is locked in the terrifying "red-room" – the room where her Uncle died. Finally she is packed off to live at Lowood School, a charitable institution for orphan girls.

The school is run by a "pompous and meddling" clergyman, Mr Brocklehurst,

> " '*Do you think, because I am poor, obscure, plain, and little, I am soulless and heartless? You think wrong! – I have as much soul as you – and full as much heart!*' "

who starves the girls in the puritanical belief that when "you feed their vile bodies . . . you starve their immortal souls".

In Jane's first year a typhus epidemic hits the school, causing a scandal that forces a beneficial change of management. Jane can now settle into a studious and contented girlhood, eventually becoming a teacher herself.

An unwanted dependant
Orphaned and moneyless, young Jane barely survives life with the bullying Reed family. She tries to escape their ire by hiding in secluded corners, immersed in fairy tales or travel books. Continually taunted and provoked – "you ought to beg, and not live here with gentlemen's children like us" – she learns how to resist. In the end, the moral victory is hers — it is the first of several stages of her self-discovery.

J. Atkinson Grimshaw: The Haunted House/Fine Art Photographic Library

Thornfield Hall
Jane leaves Lowood to seek independence as a governess at Rochester's "manor-house". The building is both homely and eerie, but her love for Rochester turns it into a "paradise" for her. A storm-struck, "iron-garthed" chestnut tree in the grounds becomes a powerful symbol of the disaster that is to first part, and then unite them.

By the age of 18, however, Jane is longing for "change, stimulus" and advertises for a post as governess. The only reply she receives takes her once more into the unknown, to Thornfield Hall. The master of the house, Mr Rochester, is away, but Jane makes friends with her pupil, Adèle (Mr Rochester's French ward), and the kindly housekeeper, Mrs Fairfax.

Out for a walk one evening, Jane encounters a ghostly dog, followed by a man on horseback. As she watches, horse and rider fall, and the vision becomes an abrupt reality. Jane offers help, and so begins her acquaintance with Mr Rochester.

Sophisticated and dominating, Mr Rochester is enchanted by Jane's piquant wit and her brave spirit, and Jane quickly feels he is a "relation" rather than a "master". Her unaccustomed happiness is marred, however, by two bizarre incidents. Rochester is nearly burned alive in his bed, and a visitor to the Hall – Richard Mason – is viciously stabbed and bitten. Each time

J. Millais, Waiting/Birmingham City Museums and Art Gallery

Calm and quiet
*Jane's developing
maturity is marked by
periods of intense
drama that burst in on
her quiet isolation. Her
master's arrival at
Thornfield shatters the
calm life she leads there.*

Society ladies
*(below) Jane possesses
a dignity much unlike
Rochester's other
lady-friends. They
pursue conventional
achievements, she is
"cast in a different
mould".*

the culprit is said to be Grace Poole, one of the servants, who lives apart in an upstairs room, from which Jane sometimes hears peals of eerie laughter.

Meanwhile, the beautiful, well-born Blanche Ingram visits the Hall, and Jane is convinced that she and Rochester will marry. Sad, but determined to suppress her love, Jane is recalled to Gateshead to tend her Aunt who is seriously ill. She dies before being reconciled with Jane.

Returning to her duties at Thornfield Hall, Jane finds Rochester waiting. He convinces her that she is the woman he loves and wants to marry.

On their wedding day, Rochester hurries Jane to the church. Just as they are about to take their vows, Mason appears and declares a lawful impediment to the marriage: that Rochester already has a wife. A mad and dangerous woman, she is kept under lock and key in the attic at Thornfield Hall. Shattered by this awful revelation, Jane flees from Thornfield Hall, having withstood Rochester's passionate pleas to become his mistress.

Now destitute, Jane wanders far from home, sleeping in the open and starving. Desperation drives her to seek food and shelter at a cosy house on the moor, and its inmates – the Reverend St John Rivers and his two sisters – befriend her.

St John is almost as charismatic as Rochester, but unlike him, is cold and earnest. When he presses Jane to join him in missionary work, she almost succumbs to the "cold, sure step" of his persuasion. On the point of agreeing to marry him, she hears a disembodied cry, " 'Jane! Jane!' ". It is Rochester's voice.

This clinches Jane's determination to see Rochester again. She returns to Thornfield Hall, only to find it a burnt-out shell, with no sign of life. She at last traces Rochester to Ferndean Manor where he lives alone – but he has altered in a way that spells a certain change in their relationship.

A SPIRITED ROMANCE

Jane Eyre is, first and foremost, a love story, and one which explores with rare honesty the complexities of passion and tenderness, of sexual love as opposed to simple affection.

The love affair between Jane and Rochester forms the core of the book, and gives it its impetus. In all its fluctuations,

> "Women are supposed to be very calm generally: but women feel just as men feel; they need exercise for their faculties and a field for their efforts as much as their brothers do;"

their love strikes the reader as real and moving, and it derives much of its credibility from the passionate and spirited character of Jane herself.

Though much in love, she refuses to be trifled with – she is any man's equal, not least Rochester's. Jane puts her case with all the pent-up intensity of someone forced into a position of dependence and insignificance. Thinking that Rochester is to reject her and marry the dazzling Blanche Ingram, she bursts out:

Do you think I am an automaton? – a machine without feelings? and can bear to have my morsel of bread snatched from my lips, and my drop of living water dashed from my cup? . . . And if God had gifted me with some beauty and much wealth, I should have made it as hard for you to leave me, as it is now for me to leave you. I am not talking to you now through the medium of custom, conventionalities, nor even of mortal flesh: it is my spirit that addresses your spirit; just as if both had passed through the grave, and we stood at God's feet equal – as we are!'

Even during their courtship, Jane is aware of the dangers of Rochester's lapses

A dutiful teacher
The shattering news that Rochester has a mad wife drives Jane to near-madness herself. She recovers to find herself among friends, and takes on the task of running the village school. At first she finds the work degrading, but she slowly wins the respect of the community and is revived by it. She finds it impossible to forget Rochester and dreams of him "always at some exciting crisis".

G. W. Brownlow: Straw Plaiting/Fine Art Photographic Library

In the Background

MISSIONARY ZEAL

Even as *Jane Eyre* was being written, David Livingstone was achieving fame as a missionary explorer. St John Rivers and Mr Brocklehurst are also types of 19th-century missionary. Many zealous men like these took the gospel of Christ to the pagans of the dark continents – and often imposed it with shocking severity. The pose of self-sacrificing missionary often concealed an overvaulting ambition to follow in Livingstone's footsteps. By 1850, such men had converted to Christianity 20,000 Indians, at least 10,000 Africans and almost all New Zealand's Maoris.

E. T. Archive

Massacre
(below) Missionaries were 'resolute' pioneers, with little sympathy for weakness in others. Some paid the price.

Gospel preaching
(above) Many remarkable men sailed away to take the gospel to the 'natives' – and to establish an empire.

E. T. Archive

Thornfield ablaze
Jane is drawn back to
Thornfield Hall – and
Rochester. She finds it
a blackened ruin
"perforated with
paneless windows".
But the tragedy contains
the seeds of Jane's
happiness – Jane is
now an independent
woman and Rochester
needs her.

into sentimentality. At one point he calls her "a very angel" and she retorts,
'Mr Rochester, you must neither expect nor exact anything celestial of me – for you will not get it, any more than I shall get it of you.'

With her tough common-sense and her "needle of repartee", Jane keeps their relationship firmly rooted in reality.

The novel is also very much Jane's story, and it concerns her passionate need to establish an identity distinct from the one thrust on her by society. Even as a browbeaten child she is angry and rebellious, and the conformity she learns at school is merely a veneer. Becoming a governess gives her a measure of independence, but her aspirations do not end there.

Rochester is the first person of authority she has encountered who does not preach the value of restraint. He wants her to be herself, not the model product of a charitable institution, and he provides gentle, and sometimes mocking, encouragement.
'. . . you fear . . . to smile too gaily, speak too freely, or move too quickly: but in time I think you will be natural with me, as I find it impossible to be conventional with you . . .'
He wants to free her nature, not dominate it, and this makes him irresistible to her.

Jane's passionate and strong-willed character leads her into moral and emotional crises, but at last secures for her the richer and more active life she desires.

REASON AND INSTINCT

Jane's progress towards maturity involves a struggle between the dictates of reason and the prompting of instinct. As a child she already knows that the harsh 'restraining' treatment inflicted on her by her Aunt Reed is brutally unjust.
'I shall remember how you thrust me back – roughly and violently thrust me back into the red-room, and locked me up there, to my dying day . . . People think you a good woman, but you are bad, hard-hearted. You are deceitful.'

Her words, not surprisingly, cause her Aunt to quail. But their unrestrained flow releases in Jane herself an almost euphoric sense of freedom and power.

The conflict between duty and passion is at its height when Jane clashes with the pious St John Rivers. Handsome, intellectually gifted but emotionally cold, St John repeatedly argues that it is Jane's duty to be his wife and accompany him in his missionary work. His stern and dominating character has an almost hypnotic effect

on her – until she realizes that he wishes only to dominate her.

Jane knows that the kind of love St John offers is soulless, for all that it is dressed up as a religious vocation.
'I scorn your idea of love . . . I scorn the counterfeit sentiment you offer: yes, St John, and I scorn you when you offer it.'

And she does so because she knows he is incapable of loving her for herself, with all her defects, and because he implies that the love he offers – a kind of dutiful affection – is a 'higher' kind. St John is therefore the antithesis of Rochester, and it is to Rochester that Jane now turns. It is no accident that, at this point, Jane imagines she hears Rochester's voice calling her. Her instinct that he is her true soul-mate has been borne out by experience.

Through the character of Jane, Charlotte Brontë wanted to expose much of the hypocrisy current at the time, and to restore the quality of human relationships. As she wrote in the preface to the second edition of *Jane Eyre,* her aim was to remind people of 'certain simple truths', that 'Conventionality is not morality. Self-righteousness is not religion.' These truths are powerfully dramatized in *Jane Eyre.*

CHARACTERS IN FOCUS

The nature of the central characters in *Jane Eyre* convey the major themes of the novel. All play their part in Jane's slow progress towards self-fulfilment. Some impede or stifle her nature, others form a clear contrast to it – only one encourages her to find her true self. Through Jane's relationships with others, Charlotte Brontë makes a passionate plea for the right to be loved without losing independence or identity.

WHO'S WHO

Jane Eyre   Heroine and narrator. A plain orphan brought up with "miserable cruelty" by her widowed Aunt Reed until sent to Lowood charity school. At 18, Jane seeks her independence and goes to work as a governess at Thornfield Hall.

The Reeds   Jane's wealthy, snobbish aunt and her three cousins, John, Eliza and Georgiana. They make Jane's early childhood lonely, bitter and loveless.

Mister Brocklehurst   Tyrannical manager of Lowood School. Full of cant, he sets out to "mortify the sin of pride". The girls in his care suffer from his frugal regime, while his family lives in luxury.

Helen Burns   Jane's friend and mentor at Lowood School. Submissive and other-worldly, Jane adores her but cannot be like her.

Edward Rochester   The master of Thornfield Hall. Experienced and imperious, he charms Jane by his very directness, and delights in her poignant wit. But he is troubled by secrets that have serious consequences for her.

Adèle Varens   Jane's pupil is Rochester's ward and the daughter of his former French mistress. An affectionate, sweet but frivolous little girl.

Bertha Mason   Rochester's violently mad wife who haunts the upper floors of Thornfield Hall.

Blanche Ingram   A haughty, beautiful aristocrat who thinks Rochester an ideal 'catch'.

St John Rivers   A clergyman of classically good looks and virtues, he tries to win Jane's heart with his cold missionary zeal.

Fine Art Photographic Library

(left) *"too vehement, too impulsive"* by her friend Helen's standards, Jane is also "quaint, quiet, grave and simple" in the eyes of Mr Rochester. All her associates cast a judgement – but the real story lies in her own search for an identity. "Cast in a different mould to the majority", she yearns for "all of incident, life, fire, feeling that I desired and had not in my actual existence". Her growth is marked by dramatic periods of self-discovery resulting from a series of conflicts with bullies and tyrants. Her moral triumphs over the Reeds, Brocklehurst and St John Rivers only help to clarify her needs and nature; "I believed in the existence of other and more vivid kinds of goodness". In other words, she craves "more than custom has pronounced necessary" for a "schoolgirl-governess".

An unyielding "black column" of tyranny, Mr Brocklehurst runs Lowood School with unfeeling rigidity and severe frugality. He rules over the girls in his charge with imperious disdain. Full of cant and hypocrisy, his "mission is to mortify in these girls the lusts of the flesh, to teach them to clothe themselves with shamefacedness". It is no small irony that while Jane seeks her true identity and nature, Brocklehurst declares that "we are not to conform to nature". His substitute is conformity to a convention of self-denial that is riddled with hypocrisy.

"pale and bloodless" Helen Burns (right) is Jane's friend and mentor at Lowood. A brilliant mind, she embodies a philosophy of submission: "revenge never worries my heart, degradation never too deeply disgusts me, injustice never crushes me too low; I live in calm, looking to the end". Her calm forbearance wins Jane's love, but Jane finds her kind of tranquillity inexpressibly sad. Helen dies in Jane's arms, avowing she will "escape great suffering".

Mr Rochester (left) *is the master* of Thornfield Hall who conceals a tragic secret. Repeatedly described as unattractive, even his "dark face, with stern features and a heavy brow" cannot deter Jane – he treats her as an equal and encourages her to express her true feelings. She loves him for simple reasons; "My help had been needed and claimed: I had given it". His tragedy becomes her road to the freedom she craves.

Blanche Ingram's eyes are "as brilliant as her jewels" but "neither she or her sister have very large fortunes". She is a conventionally beautiful society lady, and Jane quickly recognizes her as a rival in her own growing affection for Mr Rochester. Blanche's "laugh was satirical" and her "arched and haughty lip", along with her nature, give her "a mocking air" which she uses to lash Jane in particular and governesses in general – "half of them detestable, and the rest ridiculous". All Thornfield residents believe that Mr Rochester intends to marry Blanche – only Jane recognizes her shallowness and pronounces that "she could not charm him". On hearing a rumour that his fortune is small, Blanche withdraws from the contract. Mr Rochester started the rumour.

The cruel and shallow Reed family present a compelling picture of snobbery-ridden self-centredness. They are spitefully unjust to Jane. Jane's retaliation, and her moral superiority, is the first of a series of victories; "my soul began to expand, to exult, with the strangest sense of freedom, of triumph, I ever felt". She achieves self-fulfilment and happiness, they are ruined and morally bankrupt.

The "correct and classic" St John Rivers (left) is Rochester's counterpart. While Rochester is all passion and fire, Rivers is all reason and control. "A cold, cumbrous column", he stifles love to dedicate his life to missionary zeal – and almost persuades Jane to join him. But Jane realizes that to become his "helpmeet and fellow-labourer" she must become a part of him "forced to keep the fire of my nature continually low". She finally rejects him.

'A SOUL'S EXPERIENCE'

Using as her source her few, deeply felt experiences, Charlotte Brontë sought in her writing to question convention and nicety, and appeal to the reader's own hidden feelings and aspirations.

Although her output was limited, Charlotte Brontë is among the most admired and popular of English novelists. Her emotional nature, restricted by circumstance, duty and an awareness of personal shortcomings, both motivated and found expression in her writing.

Charlotte Brontë learned the writer's craft at an early age. As a child she, together with her brother and sisters, conceived and wrote about an imaginary world – the 'Great Glass Town Confederacy'. This world of daydream and fantasy paralleled the real world, but was peopled with rich, powerful and vivid characters, more vivid than any characters their restricted world could have encompassed. Whenever the Great Glass Town needed to expand, new kingdoms and characters were invented. Charlotte and Branwell created the kingdom of Angria, and Charlotte dreamed up its romances and intrigues.

She poured more words into these Angrian fictions than she ever wrote for publication, and by the age of 14 had compiled a catalogue of dramas, stories and poems, which revealed her passionate interest in sex and sexual relationships. 'Fancy and language alike run riot,' said her biographer, Elizabeth Gaskell, to produce 'wild, weird writing'.

National Portrait Gallery: Books, The Brontë Society

THE BRUSSELS EXPERIENCE

The period Charlotte Brontë spent in Brussels with Emily was to prove crucial to her, both personally and imaginatively. The unrequited passion she felt for her teacher, Monsieur Heger, kindled an overriding need to write fiction that was grounded in acute personal, and actual, experience. Although not strictly autobiographical, her novels embody, and try to come to terms with, the struggles she herself faced.

The Professor and *Villette* are the most directly related to her Brussels experience. *Villette* is a particularly moving account of a passionate woman's struggle to accept that a normal life of joy and satisfaction cannot be hers. Indeed, all Charlotte Brontë's heroines at some point undergo crises, when the intensity of their desires conflicts with a renunciation and self-denial that are forced on them by circumstances.

Charlotte Brontë's heroines are, like her, deeply emotional, full of hopes and expectations, yet they remain isolated and unfulfilled

Childhood writings
(above and left) As children, Charlotte, Branwell, Emily and Anne poured all their imaginative energy into a fantasy world of princes, wars, intrigues and romances. One of its central figures was Charlotte's hero, the Duke of Wellington (left). The stories were written in tiny, handmade books.

Isolated heroine
(right) Charlotte's heroines gather force, originality and interest as they struggle with their isolation.

A 'real life' novel
(right) Charlotte Brontë's first novel, The Professor draws directly on her own experience. In it she overcame her taste for 'ornamented and redundant' writing, and attempted for the first time to represent the lives of real men and women. It later became Villette.

Natural imagery
(far right) The seasons are often used symbolically in Charlotte's work. Jane Eyre's loveless childhood, for example, is set against a backdrop of bleak and chilling winter weather.

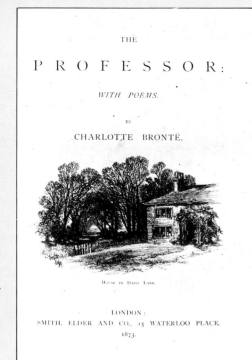

THE
PROFESSOR:
WITH POEMS.

BY

CHARLOTTE BRONTË.

HOUSE IN DAISY LANE.

LONDON:
SMITH, ELDER AND CO., 15 WATERLOO PLACE.
1873.

Nigel Blythe/Cephas

C. W. Cope: Faraway Thoughts, Christopher Wood Gallery/Bridgeman Art Library

because of their physical plainness, extreme reticence and lack of social or financial status. They attempt to overcome disappointment by channelling their passions into rigorous duty and a stern self-discipline.

Jane Eyre, Caroline Helstone in *Shirley* and Lucy Snowe in *Villette* all seek to rise above the pain of unrequited love by following the course of reason. Longing to respond to a plea for forgiveness from the man she loves, Lucy Snowe argues with herself, "'If I feel, may I never express?' 'Never!' declared Reason." But in each case, the heroine turns to reason only out of necessity, and at best it is a poor substitute for emotional fulfilment. When her heroines are 'pierced deeper' than they can endure, when they face the possibility of real love slipping from their grasp, self-control and reason is abandoned and passion is allowed its voice.

Charlotte Brontë's bitter experiences as a governess made her acutely conscious of the loneliness and vulnerability shared by so many women in the same situation. It was a career at once "'sedentary, solitary, con- strained, joyless, toilsome,'" in the words of the heroine's companion in *Shirley*.

The governess theme surfaces in all Charlotte Brontë's published novels, and its hardships are exposed with all the sharpness and sympathy of first-hand knowledge. As governesses, her heroines are socially isolated, reduced to observing rather than participating actively in life.

INNER BEAUTY

For Charlotte Brontë's heroines, the sense of being barred from life is accentuated by their unattractiveness. Jane Eyre and Lucy Snowe find their plainness an obstacle to true social acceptance, made worse by their acute self-consciousness. But although beauty is acknowledged as a passport to an easier life, the author shares with her heroines a puritanical distrust of surface appearance. The inner qualities of a character, the achievement of 'moral beauty', are her, and their, concerns.

In discussion with her sisters, Charlotte Brontë thought them 'wrong – even morally wrong – in making their heroines beautiful

19

as a matter of course'. And in her novels, she set out quite deliberately to show that though outwardly insignificant, a heroine could still be fascinating through the force of her soul. She was likewise against having editions of her books illustrated on the grounds that 'my personages are most unattractive in look'.

Charlotte Brontë's popularity, then and now, rests to a large extent on her timeless portrayal of love. Love stories dominate *Jane Eyre* and *Villette* and provide the central interest in *Shirley*. As the love gathers force, the reader is swept into the world of the heroine, pitched from hope to despair to hope again by the dramatic tension which the author creates.

Much of the tension is due to the oppositions she explores, for example between male and female qualities within one character. Mr Rochester may be brusque and masculine to an extreme, but he is also tender and passionate. Similarly, her heroines are creatures of contrast, at once reticent and forceful.

THE PUBLIC'S REACTION
What delighted Charlotte Brontë's readers and outraged some critics was not her choice of women as central characters, but the nature of those women. In laying bare her heroine's inner life she showed a degree of psychological honesty and vigour that was considered coarse and 'fierce'.

The unrestrained force of passion in her heroines was condemned by some, and prompted the author Harriet Martineau to state of *Villette*, 'I do not like the love, either the kind or the degree of it'.

The publication of *Jane Eyre* secured for Charlotte Brontë a huge and eager readership. 'Public taste seems to have outstripped its guides' in realizing her 'remarkable power', wrote one critic. At the same time as paying tribute to her 'piquancy and originality', many critics were uncomfortably aware that here was a mind uncompromising in its integrity. *Jane Eyre* was called a 'dangerous book' and its author 'soured, coarse and grumbling'. Even the poet Matthew Arnold could find 'nothing but hunger, rebellion and rage' in the mind of the author of *Villette*.

If there is 'rage' in Charlotte Brontë's books, it is rage against the humiliations and frustrations endured by many women of her class, and the narrow choices open to them. The critics were perhaps shocked by the way in which her heroines disregard convention, but Charlotte Brontë was consciously opposed to what was evil about the conventions of her time.

All her heroines have qualities of endurance, courage and forcefulness to equal a man's, yet all are denied self-fulfilment by the confined society in which they live. Her express intention was to show that women's

feelings and needs should be taken as seriously as men's had always been.

It was partly because 'authoresses are liable to be looked on with prejudice', as she put it, that made Charlotte Brontë use a pseudonym. She wanted to be judged as a writer without her sex intruding. She was aware, too, that the work of female authors was judged by far lower standards than the work of men. Above all, though, she wanted to avoid any personal publicity for herself and her sisters.

A POSSESSED WRITER
Unlike many other Victorian novelists, Charlotte Brontë did not make writing a daily ritual. In fact, 'sometimes weeks or even months elapsed' before she felt able to continue a novel. At other times, however, she would wake up with the next part of her story 'clear and bright' in her mind. Such was the power of her imagination that at times like this she was 'possessed', and the imaginary incidents became more real to her than 'her actual life itself'.

Charlotte Brontë wrote her first draft in pencil on tiny sheets of notepaper, resting on a piece of cardboard as an improvised desk. She had to hold this close to her eyes, because she was so shortsighted. Thus she was able to write as she sat near the fire, or in bed.

The Brontë Society

Poetic justice *(above) In* Jane Eyre, *Charlotte Brontë exposes her former teacher, the Reverend Carus Wilson. A man 'willing to sacrifice everything but power', like Mr. Brocklehurst.*

A "shower of curates" *(below) The pages of* Shirley *contain a veritable rogues' gallery of clergymen – a type which Charlotte Brontë portrays with amusing and unsparing wit.*

David Messum Fine Paintings/Bridgeman Art Library

Simon Warner

Afterwards, she would copy out the final version in a delicate, legible hand.

In her dealings with publishers, she was both business-like and shrewd. Despite her timidity, she had a strongly independent mind. 'I must have my own way in the matter of writing' she told a publisher, and she declined to revise any novel once it was finished. Her one exception was to make the tragic end of *Villette* more muted – in deference to her father's wishes.

With the exception of *Shirley*, Charlotte Brontë's novels use a first-person narrative, the events being seen through the eyes of the main character. This device considerably heightens the unity and intensity of her work, and imbues the settings and natural descriptions with the narrator's state of mind – making them both vividly real while powerfully imaginative. In the words of the Victorian critic G.H. Lewes, her evocations of nature 'were all painted to your *soul* as well as to your eyes'.

POETIC IMAGINATION

Throughout her novels, natural imagery is used symbolically. Natural events often foretell or accompany changes or disasters in the human sphere. In *Villette*, the heroine's near-breakdown occurs against a backdrop of "raging storm and beating rain". The tragic end is suggested solely through images of flaming, "bloody" skies and storms frenzied enough to cause a shipwreck.

Yet alongside this dramatic, moody imagery runs a keen attention to detail, which imparts the atmosphere of the actual world. There is the vivid flavour of daily life in the Belgian school in *Villette* – the smell of coffee and rolls, the 'tartines' and baked pears, the wooden school desks and the dormitories.

Concerned more that her words should be a truthful mirror of her thoughts than that she should write beautifully, Charlotte used slang expressions, phrases in French and provincial idioms to convey her exact meaning.

According to Mrs Gaskell, she 'never wrote down a sentence until she clearly understood what she wanted to say, had deliberately chosen the words and arranged them in their right order'. Her intention is clear, but critics found much to condemn in her free flow of language, considering it vulgar in its use of Yorkshire dialect, or affected in its scattering of French.

When real experience is transformed by her creative imagination, Charlotte Brontë achieves and sustains a rare poetic intensity. But at all times, her work is marked by authentic feeling. What G.H. Lewes wrote of *Jane Eyre* holds true for all her writing: 'From out of the depths of a sorrowing experience, here was a voice speaking to the experience of thousands.'

Local settings
(above) Although she travelled little, Charlotte's few visits away from home provided her with useful background material for her writing. Thus, a Lancashire manor house (shown here), the Peak district and her own moorland scenery all find their way into her work.

Eminent admirer
(right) Jane Eyre won for its author the praise of key literary figures, not least of whom was the novelist, William Thackeray. Charlotte dedicated the second edition of Jane Eyre to him, little knowing that he, like Rochester, had an insane wife.

National Portrait Gallery

Cornhill, London
(right) Charlotte visited her publishers Smith, Elder several times, and they introduced her to London. She found such visits 'an exciting whirl' to which she was peculiarly unaccustomed. But Smith and his mother were unfailingly kind to her, even attempting to hide an adverse review of Shirley which had appeared.

Mansell Collection

WORKS·IN OUTLINE

Author of only four completed novels and some poems, Charlotte Brontë is regarded as one of the greatest writers on human passion. The success of *Jane Eyre* was followed by *Villette* and *Shirley*; her first novel, *The Professor* appearing after her death. Charlotte's first published work was a selection of *Poems*, which included works by her sisters. Charlotte's own poems are simple in form and largely autobiographical, embodying the ideas she was to explore more deeply in her novels.

VILLETTE
◆ 1853 ◆

Villette is the most sustained of Charlotte Brontë's novels, and the most openly autobiographical, using the same subject matter as *The Professor*. Its heroine, Lucy Snowe (below right) – friendless, and plain – is a teacher in the fictitious Belgian town of Villette. Her acute self-consciousness and fear of rejection conflict with her passionate nature, but give her an unusual air of self-assurance. Her isolation, and her own sense of being cast in a different mould, is intensified by the showy Catholicism of her environment, which is so alien to her own puritan nature. Recognizing that her love for the English doctor, John Bretton, will never be returned, Lucy withdraws even more. Gradually, she transfers her unrequited love to Paul Emmanuel (below), the school's professor – a despotic, irascible man much older than Lucy. Nevertheless, he is profoundly passionate and kind, and their relationship, though unorthodox, brings them both happiness. It is shattered when he is obliged to go the West Indies, but Lucy is left in charge of the school, awaiting his return. Lucy's experiences are made intensely real, and the minor characters are superbly drawn – notably the manipulative headmistress, Madame Beck, and the pretty Ginevra Fanshawe (right), with whom John Bretton is infatuated. The great Victorian novelist, George Eliot, valued *Villette* even more highly than *Jane Eyre*.

Fine Art Photographic Library

City of York Art Gallery/Bridgeman Art Library

R. Redgrave: The Governess/Victoria and Albert Museum

SHIRLEY
◆ 1849 ◆

Charlotte Brontë's most socially aware novel, *Shirley* is set in Yorkshire during the Luddite riots. The riots were popularly supported – the labour-intensive wool industry was in decline and industrialization was threatening jobs and driving the dispossessed to desperation. The plot revolves around four main characters: Shirley Keeldar (left), an heiress; Caroline Helstone, a gentle retiring young woman obliged to look after her elderly uncle (below); Robert Moore, a determined mill-owner who persists in introducing labour-saving machinery (below, left); and his brother Louis, tutor to the Keeldar family. Its recurrent theme is a sustained protest against the narrow life to which poor, single women – like Caroline – are condemned. By contrast, the strong, independent Shirley is able to control her destiny. She rejects the offer of an expedient marriage to Robert, but finally accepts and returns Louis' love. Despite the important place that love occupies in the novel, Charlotte Brontë set out to make it as "unromantic as Monday morning". It is thus a new departure for her, in being concerned not solely with inner drama and conflict, but with 'a piece of actual life'. She researched into the historical background, and drew even her minor characters from life, while Shirley herself is modelled on her beloved and much admired sister, Emily.

The strongest elements of *Jane Eyre* are still to be found in this later novel – independent and spirited heroines; the narrow lot of conventional womanhood; mismatched affections and attractions; charismatic and powerful male characters. And it also contains similar touches of melodrama and unlikely coincidences; Mrs Pryor, Shirley's one-time governess, turns out to be Caroline's long-lost mother. But the most memorable theme, and its source, could be said to be sisterhood itself.

The Impoverished Gentlewoman

**A woman with gentility but no money was out of place
in Victorian society. She had to work to survive, but most of the
ladylike options open to her were ill-paid and humiliating.**

would be taken over by another man and the sisters would face destitution. It must have been clear at an early date that drunken, erratic Branwell Brontë would never be able to support any of his sisters.

The fact that Patrick Brontë – already 60 when Charlotte reached the age of 21 – outlived every one of his children could not have been predicted, and made no difference to the way they viewed their prospects when girls. Haworth parsonage remained a refuge for them all their lives.

One obvious option for the impoverished gentlewoman was to live with relatives. Sometimes she was welcome and wanted, but the impoverished single relative might also become the family drudge, made humiliatingly aware of her dependency, as little Jane Eyre is by her bullying cousin John Reed: "You are a dependant, Mamma says, you have no money; your father left you none; you ought to beg, and not to live here with gentlemen's children like us."

Along with thousands of other women, Charlotte Brontë and her sisters were the victims of a characteristic 19th-century dilemma. They were too poor to live without working, yet they were also ladies, a fact that severely limited what decent society would allow them to do without loss of caste. Paradoxically, almost all ladylike employments were ill-paid, stressful and humiliating.

In theory, gentility and wealth went hand in hand, but in reality there were many women who were obviously genteel and yet lacked money of their own or a man to maintain them. Often ladies came down in the world because the family fortunes collapsed in the still-unstable circumstances of early Victorian enterprise, characterized by alternating speculative manias and bank failures, booms and slumps. Victorian novels are full of financial catastrophes. In *Agnes Grey,* by Charlotte Brontë's sister Anne, speculations ruin the heroine's father and force her out into the world as a governess.

Less sensationally, the children of more poorly paid professional men – such as Charlotte's Cambridge-educated clergyman father – were faced with poverty if the breadwinner became incapable or died. Cramped as the early lives of the Brontë sisters were, their prospects must have seemed even more alarming. If Mr Brontë died, the parsonage

The trials of teaching
(above left) Many educated but poor gentlewomen earned a pitiful salary teaching in charity schools as did Jane Eyre. Like her, many must often have felt "degraded" and "dismayed".

The poor seamstress
(above right) Dressmaking seemed a 'genteel' occupation for a respectable woman but, in reality, it was desperately unrewarding work – employment was insecure, the hours dreadful and the wages minimal.

Marriage prospects
(right) One of the few ways a poor gentlewoman could escape the trap of poverty and degradation was through marriage. Any caring father would scrutinize the financial standing of a prospective husband very carefully.

Nineteenth-century writers were quite certain that marriage was the norm, and the proper goal for any healthy woman. They also recognized that genteel poverty was an evil. Yet, inconsistently, they scorned husband-hungry girls and their man-trapping mothers. One of the most famous examples in 19th-century literature is the foolish Mrs Bennet in Jane Austen's *Pride and Prejudice,* who can think of nothing except finding husbands for her five daughters. Yet her marital scheming could just as easily have been presented as caring and commonsense. To the impoverished gentle-woman, marriage meant release from the threat of poverty or, at worst, a sharing of burdens.

ESCAPE INTO MARRIAGE

Although most marriages were no longer 'arranged' by families, many were negotiated with at least half an eye on practicalities – hence Mr Rochester's unfortunate contract with Bertha Mason in *Jane Eyre.* A poor gentlewoman might have chances if she was prepared to ignore personal inclination. When Charlotte Brontë received a proposal from Henry Nussey, the curate told her plainly that he was about to take in pupils and needed a wife to look after them. When St John Rivers proposes to Jane Eyre, he wants a loyal helper in his missionary work. Both the fictional and the real offers were refused, but there were plenty of girls who were more down-to-earth in their expectations. Henry Nussey soon found a wife to fulfil his needs.

Marriage had severe drawbacks for a woman of independent spirit, whether impoverished or not. A husband became the master of her person, and

The abandoned mother

(above) Solitary women were prey to 'adventurers' who played upon their need to find security through marriage. Seamstresses for rich households were especially vulnerable – there were countless untold tragedies of seduced women abandoned with an illegitimate child.

Elizabeth Gaskell

(above) Charlotte Brontë's friend and biographer, the novelist Mrs Gaskell, was one of the fortunate few women whose literary talents allowed them to earn a living respectably – but even she was obliged to work at the dining room table so that her husband could occupy the study.

also of her property and income – a situation only remedied by Married Women's Property Acts from 1870 onwards. A wife was expected to submit to her husband's will, adopt his opinions and run the household in such a way that he remained free from its worries. Although Charlotte's friend and biographer Mrs Gaskell was a celebrated novelist, it was her husband who occupied the study – she wrote her novels on the dining room table, from which she could monitor the servants and children.

Charlotte Brontë, already a famous writer when she married, allowed Arthur Bell Nicholls to interfere in her correspondence with Ellen Nussey, and

Accomplished ladies
(below, left and right)
Young ladies were expected to play the piano and sketch prettily. Jane Eyre can play "like any other English schoolgirl" but, as Rochester recognizes, she is an artist of rare talent. Yet neither Jane nor any other lady could respectably exploit her talent – the best she could hope for was to teach.

In London and other cities the demand for her services was tremendous but concentrated: during 'the season' she sewed for an average of 18 hours a day, whereas her working day during the rest of the year was a only 12 hours. The hardship and penury – contrasted with the often glamorous contacts they made – quite often led to seduction, followed by a rapid descent into prostitution.

The murky moral and economic facts about dressmaking were repeatedly exposed by Victorian writers such as Thomas Hood, whose poem 'The Song of a Shirt' had a tremendous vogue. Such exposés did little to improve the seamstress's lot,

in the last few months of her life spent more time on her husband's parish duties than in her creative writing. Real life was rather different from the fictitious world of *Jane Eyre*, where it is the man who becomes a helpless dependant, or of *The Professor* and *Villette,* where the heroines retain their independence as teachers to the very last page.

A WOMAN'S PLACE

'The female sphere' – a woman's proper place – was the home, whether she ruled as its mistress or laboured in it as a servant. Genteel work outside the home was almost non-existent: public office, the professions and the universities were all closed to women, while commerce and manual labour were simply not respectable.

If 'reduced ladies driven to obtain a maintenance' wished to retain their gentility, they had to do 'women's work' in a setting as domestic as possible. Of employments now thought of as 'traditionally' feminine and respectable, even nursing was out of the question; nurses were working-class women with bad reputations until Florence Nightingale's reforms took effect in the 1860s.

Some gentlewomen worked as seamstresses, although the profession was mainly recruited from girls who belonged to a lower social class (like Mrs Gaskell's Mary Barton) and were attracted by the seeming gentility of dressmaking. In reality, the seamstress was pitifully paid and overworked.

H. Brooker: The Treasured Volume/Fine Art Photographic Library

but they effectively discouraged gentlewomen, who rarely took up this kind of work.

At the other extreme, literature held out the possibility of an extraordinary advance in affluence and status, if only for the lucky and talented few. Not all men approved: when Charlotte Brontë turned to the poet Robert Southey for advice, he told her that 'Literature cannot be the business of a woman's life, and it ought not to be', and that her household duties should take up all her time. Charlotte's beloved teacher, 'Monsieur', was equally negative about a writing career.

But these were rather old-fashioned views. Women had long been accepted as novelists, partly because the novel itself was originally regarded as a lightweight literary form requiring no great knowledge or talent. Writing continued to be a respectable profession for ladies, partly because it could be carried out at home – though by the 19th century, great restrictions had been placed on the language and subject matter permitted to writers of both sexes, and to women in particular. One good reason for the Brontë's pseudonyms was given by Mary Ann Evans, who herself wrote as 'George Eliot': 'The object of anonymity was to get the book judged on its own merits, and not prejudged as the work of a woman'.

THE VICTORIAN GOVERNESS

Although Charlotte eventually joined the ranks of the famous – and potentially rich – her earlier work experience was identical to that of most other impoverished gentlewomen: she was engaged as governess. Governesses included what we now call teachers; women who worked in charity or boarding schools. Standards in these institutions varied greatly. Charlotte and Emily Brontë taught at Yorkshire schools in the mid 1830s, but the work was virtually slave labour.

To obtain a decent position – or better still, to run a school of one's own – required a more systematic education than most gentlewomen acquired. This was why Charlotte and Emily studied at the Pensionnat Heger in Brussels – its value was proved by the fact that a large Manchester boarding school later offered Charlotte the post of 'first governess' for the magnificent sum of £100 per annum. Because of her father's ill-health, Charlotte refused; but her novel, *Villette,* ends on a note of wish-fulfilment, with Lucy Snowe as an independent professional woman in charge of her own school.

By contrast, Charlotte's salary as the White family's 'private governess' – that is, live-in teacher and child minder – was a mere £20 a year, with £4 deducted for laundry. She was not cut out for the work. She did not care for small children, liking only Mr White because 'He never asks me to wipe the children's smutty noses or tie their shoes or fetch their pinafores or set them a chair'. And she complained that Mrs White 'cares nothing in the world about me except to contrive how the greatest quantity of labour may be squeezed out of me, and to that end she overwhelms me with oceans of needlework, yards of cambric to hem, muslin

A solitary life
(above) Life for the governess was often intensely lonely, lived in a limbo between master and servants, excluded from friendship with either. Jane Eyre's experience at Thornfield Hall is typical – the governess hears all the fun, but cannot join in: " . . . light steps ascended the stairs; and there was a tripping through the gallery, and soft cheerful laughs, and opening and closing doors and, for a time, hush".

Women together
(left) Although working class women were often much worse off materially than even the impoverished gentlewoman, many at least had the fellowship of other women. This contemporary picture shows women millworkers in Wigan together during a break.

27

nightcaps to make, and, above all things, dolls to dress'. Others were similarly treated.

As well as being underpaid and overworked, the governess suffered from the contradictions inherent in her position. She was a lady, admitted to the drawing and dining rooms when her employees wanted to show her off, and too good to eat or associate with even the upper servants (whose salaries were nonetheless at least as large as hers). But she was also an employee, and as such must be prepared to endure brusque treatment and severe rebukes. She had to make herself unobtrusive so that her mistress should not feel rivalled.

CONTINUAL SLIGHTS

Even the governess's authority over the children was insecure, since she had no power to discipline them without the mistress's consent; and even if they were 'riotous, perverse, unmanageable cubs', like the little Sidgwicks who Charlotte Brontë was employed to tame, their mother was too often inclined to make excuses for them while resenting the trouble she was being caused.

Charlotte's resentment of the slights she endured as a governess are reflected in *Jane Eyre* – for example when Mr Rochester's beautiful 'fiancée' Blanche Ingram recounts (in Jane's hearing) the cruel fun that she and her brother had at their governess's expense:

But poor Madame Joubert! I see her yet in her raging passions, when we had driven her to extremities – spilt our tea, crumbled our bread and butter, tossed our books up to the ceiling, and played a charivari with the ruler and the desk, the fender and the fire irons. Theodore, do you remember those merry days?'

'Yaas, to be sure I do,' drawled Lord Ingram; 'and the poor old stick used to cry out, "Oh you villains childs!" and then we sermonized her on the presumption of attempting to teach such clever blades as we were, when she was herself so ignorant.'

This catalogue of woes does not just come from Charlotte Brontë's writing. Her sister Anne, who worked as a governess for seven years, gives a similar account in *Agnes Grey*. And non-fictional evidence proves that the governess's life was singularly isolated and stressful.

The low salaries received by governesses ensured that those who outlived their usefulness would save little or nothing, and end their days in the workhouse. However, Victorian novels and reports did encourage public concern, and in 1843 the Governesses' Benevolent Institution was founded. It set up a Home for those in temporary difficulties, awarded annuities to aged governesses, and kept a register of available employment. But more important in the long run was the founding of Queen's College in London.

This was intended to give governesses a proper training, but it was soon flooded with women eager to improve themselves, including some of the future pioneers of education for women. Their work, and the wider job opportunities provided by social change and intelligent agitation, began the transformation of impoverished gentlewomen into educated, efficient women.

Nursing the sick
Surprisingly perhaps, even nursing the sick was not considered suitable work for a respectable lady. In Charlotte Brontë's day, nurses generally had a rather dubious reputation. It took the efforts of Florence Nightingale – shown here tending the wounded in the Crimea, 1856 – to elevate the status of nursing.

A sign of improvement
(below) Towards the end of the 19th century, the lot of the poor gentlewoman began to improve, with the establishment of institutions such as Queen's College in London. This was set up to give governesses a proper training, but many others took advantage of it.

EMILY BRONTË

← 1818-1848 →

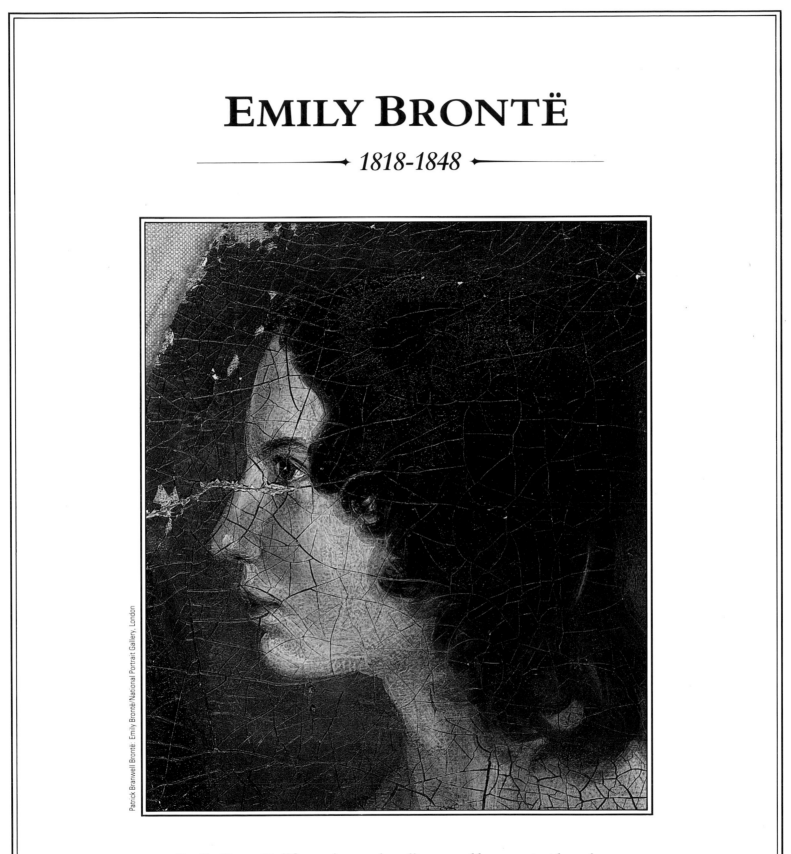

Emily Brontë's life was intensely solitary: and her greatest happiness
was in roaming her native moors alone. Emily's extraordinary
courage and inability to compromise resulted in one of the most
passionate, violent and controversial books of the 19th century, and a
unique body of poetry, all published shortly before her early death.
As D. H. Lawrence wrote, '. . . life does not mean length of days.
Poor old Queen Victoria had length of days. But Emily Brontë had
life. She died of it.'

"No Coward Soul"

Life was never easy for Emily Brontë. Only alone on the moors, surrounded by the familiar sights of her private world, could she find peace and inspiration.

The life of Emily Brontë was short, intense and led in almost total seclusion. All that we know of her is what she reveals in her poems, and her single novel, *Wuthering Heights*, and what has been left in the recorded memoirs of the few who knew her. Her sister Charlotte is a major source of information, but for some reason she destroyed many of Emily's papers after her death and suppressed the most significant aspect of her – that she was a mystic who drew inspiration not from what she called 'the World without', but from visions and moments of intense emotion when she felt a oneness with Nature and the immaterial Universe. These fleeting moments were to provide her greatest happiness and were what gave shape to her life, her thought, and her work.

Emily Jane Brontë was born on 30 July 1818 at Thornton parsonage in the parish of Bradford in Yorkshire. Two years younger than Charlotte, and a year younger than her brother Branwell, Emily was closest to her younger sister Anne, who was to be her dearest friend and confidante.

In character and temperament, she seems to have had much in common with her father, Patrick Brontë, a Celt with a vivid imagination, strong literary tastes and a forceful, unbending personality. Of her mother, Emily knew or remembered nothing, being only three when she died of cancer at the age of 38, leaving six children. The family's 'mother-figure' was to become their Aunt Branwell, a well-meaning, but nevertheless stern and undemonstrative woman.

In 1824, Emily joined her sisters Charlotte, Maria and Elizabeth at Cowan Bridge school. Though Maria and Elizabeth were to die of tuberculosis, and Charlotte was marred for life by the experience, Emily seems to have been surprisingly unaffected. As the youngest pupil, she was seen as 'a darling child', 'quite the pet nursling of the school', and was protected from the grim, miserable reality of the place.

Returning to Haworth after an absence of six months, Emily remained at home for the next ten years. Though tutored by her father, from whom she acquired a passion for poetry, she grew up free from

The Reverend Brontë
(right) Of all the children, Emily was the most similar to her father in temperament. He, too, was intensely private and an awesome personality. Throughout his long life he ate his meals alone, engendering equal stoicism and detachment in his children.

Yorkshire landscape
(below) In her cherished Haworth, Emily could escape to the moors. They were her refuge and her playground, and she loved the windy heights, the soft heathers and the inexorable flow of the seasons.

Pastoral quietude
The beautiful setting of Thornton was just 8 miles from Haworth, where the Brontës moved to in 1820. Of all the influences on Emily's life, the landscape of her childhood was to have the most profound effect on her art.

Barnaby's Picture Library

Emily's birthplace
All six Brontë children were born at the Thornton vicarage in the parish of Bradford. Emily Jane Brontë was the fifth, born on 30 July 1818. Anne, who was to become her lifelong friend and confidante, was born there 18 months later.

The Brontë Society

many of the restrictions normally placed on children.

Under the watchful eye of Tabitha Aykroyd, 'Tabby', a widow of 56 employed at the parsonage as housekeeper, Emily would roam up to 20 miles a day over the moors, returning home at night to the austere little parsonage and the bed she shared with Charlotte. During these walks, her imagination was fed with tales of the supernatural told by Tabby whose memory stretched back to the turbulent times of the old century.

MAGICAL SOLDIERS

Not long after the girls returned from Cowan Bridge, Patrick Brontë bought a box of toy soldiers for Branwell. It was one of the most important events of the children's lives. Each sister chose a soldier. According to Charlotte, Emily's was dubbed 'Gravey' because the face of the little soldier was so very grave. But Branwell wrote that Emily called him 'Parry', after the Arctic explorer Captain Edward Parry. Certainly Emily was later to weave tales around 'Parrysland', a never-never land bearing a marked resemblance to Yorkshire.

Soon the Brontë children were writing stories based on the adventures of their adopted characters, jointly in the 'Glass Town' epic. Charlotte and Branwell later paired off to produce the sagas of 'Angria', while Emily and Anne created the 'Gondal' chronicles. First formulated at the age of 12, the Gondals were to sustain Emily for the rest of her life. Indeed, as the years went by, Emily increasingly inhabited the fantasy world created by her own imagination.

Excruciatingly shy in public, she rarely uttered a

The Brontë Society

Derek Forss

Key Dates

1818 born at Thornton, Yorkshire

1820 family moves to Haworth parsonage

1821 death of mother

1824 attends Cowan Bridge school

1825 death of sisters Maria and Elizabeth

1826 Patrick Brontë brings home 12 wooden soldiers

1831 begins 'Gondal'

1835 pupil at Roe Head school

1837 governess at Law Hill school, Halifax

1842 pupil at Pensionnat Heger, Brussels

1846 *Poems by Currer, Ellis and Acton Bell*, published

1847 *Wuthering Heights* published

1848 Branwell's death, followed by Emily's

ANNE BRONTË

The youngest of the Brontë children, Anne has tended to be neglected, overshadowed by her more forceful sisters and brother. Yet her two novels *Agnes Grey* and *The Tenant of Wildfell Hall*, show her to have been a frank, independent and forthright personality. "Such talents as God has given me", she wrote, "I will endeavour to put to their greatest to use."

Forced to live a life she loathed – that of governess – she nevertheless suffered it in silence. But her experience led her to become a feminist at a time when the word was unknown, claiming equal rights for women.

Under her reticent exterior, Anne hid a deeply passionate nature. The love that she formed for her father's curate, Willie Weightman, she could only express after his death. She was to mourn her loss until her own death, from consumption, five months after Emily's in 1849.

The Brontë Society

Talented sisters
Last but not least in the Brontë family, Anne was the subject of Charlotte's portrait (above) and collaborated with Emily on her diaries (left).

word to strangers or even to those to whom she had been introduced. On the rare occasions when Emily was thrown into the company of people outside the family circle, Charlotte's constant anxious question was, 'How did Emily behave?' Often she remained totally silent when spoken to.

DESPERATELY HOMESICK

Charlotte, and even the timid Anne, adapted sufficiently to become governesses and live (albeit unhappily) away from home. Not so Emily. When, at the age of 17, she went as a pupil to Roe Head school, at which Charlotte was a teacher, it proved virtually impossible for her. Writing 15 years after the event, Charlotte said of her sister, 'Liberty was the breath of Emily's nostrils, without it, she perished . . . Every morning when she woke, the vision of home and the moors rushed on her . . . her health was quickly broken . . . I felt in my heart she would die if she did not go home . . .' After an absence of only three months, Emily returned to Haworth – where she revived in spirit and in health.

But gradually and relentlessly the shadows began to darken and close in on Emily and her family. At home, feeling herself to be a failure, she was thrown almost exclusively into the company of Branwell, a failure of Byronic intensity. Inevitably, the two drew closer together.

Increasingly she herself withdrew further from the world, despising its cruelty and meaningless social conventions. Only in the world of Nature, in the silent, seemingly self-contained world of animals, did she feel any sense of affinity. Not surprisingly, she sought companionship and solace from her ever-increasing band of pets – pigeons, pheasants, geese, her dogs Grasper and Keeper, her Merlin hawk Hero, together with numerous cats.

When Aunt Branwell threatened to expel Keeper unless he was properly house-trained, Emily beat the

obstinate beast about the head with her bare hands until, bloody and bruised, his spirit broke and he obeyed his mistress. Her own spirit and strength of will were indomitable, her physical courage phenomenal. Bitten by a suspected rabid dog she cauterized the wound with red-hot tongs.

Apart from her household duties – cooking, baking bread and managing household affairs – she taught herself German, played the piano and wrote her poetry. It was a quiet, simple, secluded life, 'all tight and right' as she described it in a Diary Paper of 1837. Yet there was a dark side to her nature, a feeling of inadequacy coupled with her feeling of separateness. 'Terrifically

Pensionnat Heger
(below) In 1842 Charlotte and Emily enrolled at the Pensionnat Heger in Brussels. Both girls worked hard: Charlotte because of her hunger for knowledge; Emily because she refused to fail. M. Heger was to say of her that her head for logic and her capability for argument were extraordinary – particularly in a woman.

The Brontë Society

and idiotically and brutally STUPID', is the harsh judgement she passed on herself. In a poem written in the same year, when she was 18, which begins:

I am the only being whose doom
No tongue would ask, no eye would mourn;

she wrote:

'Twas grief enough to find mankind
All hollow, servile, insincere;
But worse to trust to my own mind
And find the same corruption there.

It was in that same year, 1837, that Emily made another attempt at living in the world. She went as governess to the Law Hill school, Halifax. It was a desperate, unhappy attempt. To her friend Ellen Nussey, Charlotte wrote 'I have had one letter from her [Emily] since her departure . . . it gives an appalling account of her duties – hard labour from six in the morning until near eleven at night, with only one half-hour of exercise between. This is slavery. I fear she will never stand it'.

Returning to Haworth on 24 April 1838, Emily remained at home for the next four years. Although Charlotte and Anne were to take up appointments as governesses and Branwell attempted to stave off his accelerating decline, Emily followed the old routine becoming more indispensable around the house as Tabby grew less active.

Alone in the tiny old nursery room she created her own world. The room was simply furnished, with a low armchair in which she wrote, and a camp-bed pushed across the window from which at night she could gaze at the moon and the stars. There was no fireplace in the room or any form of heating. Comfort or physical ease were things she disregarded.

With the declining health of Patrick Brontë and the loneliness and isolation felt by both Charlotte and Anne, who were both living as governesses, a plan was conceived that would help the family fortunes and unite the sisters under one roof. They would set up a school of their own. Aunt Branwell agreed to finance the venture, and it was decided that Charlotte and Emily should attend a school on the Continent to perfect their French and improve their German. Their choice fell on the Pensionnat Heger in Brussels.

STUDYING ABROAD

What Emily Brontë made of it all we do not know. She left no record of her journey from the Yorkshire moors to London, the Channel crossing and arrival at Brussels. We know nothing from her own pen of her impressions of the Roman Catholic school into which she was plunged, her view of the school's proprietors, Monsieur and Madame Heger, or of the giggling girls with whom she was thrown into contact. All we have are the recollections of Charlotte as told to her biographer Mrs Gaskell, the testimony of M. Heger himself and a memoir of a former pupil, Laetitia Wheelwright.

From Mrs Gaskell we learn that 'Emily had taken a fancy to the fashion, ugly and preposterous even during its reign, of gigot sleeves, and persisting in wearing them long after they were 'gone out'. Her petticoats, too, had not a curve or wave in them, but hung straight and long, clinging to her lank figure.' To Mrs Gaskell we also owe M. Heger's opinion of Emily as 'egotistical

Haworth parsonage
(above) From 1820, the Brontë home was a Georgian house, finely proportioned but small for such a large household. The five bedrooms had to serve the Rev. and Mrs Brontë, their six children, two servants and, until her death, Mrs Brontë's nurse. The four eldest girls slept together in a room that was barely sufficient for one.

Devoted friend
Emily drew her beloved dog Keeper on the day she returned to Haworth in April 1838. Fiercely protective of his mistress, he tended to terrorize visitors and accepted dominion only from Emily.

Merlin hawk
Emily always seemed more comfortable in the company of animals than people, and by 1841 her 'family' included not just dogs but also a cat, two tame geese and a hawk. Clearly sensing an affinity with the bird, she spent long hours studying and sketching it, and honoured it in verse:
"And like myself lone, wholly lone, It sees the day's long sunshine glow; And like myself it makes its moan In unexhausted woe."

and exacting', exercising 'a kind of unconscious tyranny over' Charlotte. And from Laetitia Wheelwright we are told that Emily was a 'tallish, ungainly ill-dressed figure . . . always answering our jokes with "I wish to be as God made me" . . .'

These are unflattering, humourless portraits. One can only guess from the evidence of the poems and comments from Charlotte's letters at Emily's unhappiness, but utter determination not to fail this time. 'Emily works like a horse' noted Charlotte in a letter to Ellen Nussey, and we know that M. Heger had the highest opinion of Emily's intellectual powers.

PASSIONATELY PRIVATE

Emily had been in Brussels nine months when Aunt Branwell died. She returned to Haworth immediately to look after her father, now almost totally blind. With Anne and Charlotte away, she was mistress of the house, free to come and go as she pleased. Her poetic powers reached new heights of expression.

In 1845 her self-contained life at home was invaded by the return of Branwell. And for the next three years, Emily witnessed his daily disintegration, unable to help, incapable of averting his inevitable end. Anne returned home that same year, as did the unhappy Charlotte, suffering the pangs of an unrequited love for M. Heger.

In September or October 1845 Charlotte happened to find two rather scruffy note-books, one bearing the heading, 'Emily Jane Brontë, GONDAL POEMS'. The other also consisted of flimsy, poor-quality paper, on which were written poems of a more personal nature. Charlotte was immediately struck by their quality. These were 'not at all like the poetry women generally wrote. I thought them condensed and terse, vigorous and genuine.'

This 'discovery' of Charlotte's was something that Emily found almost unbearable. Flying into a violent

Fact or Fiction

A SIMILAR STORY

While at Law Hill, Emily heard a story remarkably like *Wuthering Heights*. It concerned an orphan, Jack Sharp, who was adopted by Mr Walker of Walterclough Hall. The boy grew up arrogant and cunning, gradually taking over the Walker business.

On Mr Walker's death in 1771, the eldest son John, egged on by his wife, claimed his rights as heir. Reluctantly, Sharp left, promising revenge. Building Law Hill a mile away, he enticed the easy-going John into gambling and ruined him. He also corrupted Sam Stead, a relative of Walker's, who later disrupted the Walker household, teaching their children foul language.

Also, Jack Sharp's manservant was called Joseph, and the Walker children's nurse, like Ellen Dean, had frequent clashes with Sharp.

***High Withens, Haworth Moor** is thought to be the original Wuthering Heights.*

Shibden Hall

(right) In 1837, Emily took a post as governess at Law Hill, a girls' boarding school on one of the Pennine hills surrounding Halifax. Although it was not a happy time for her, it was not without its distractions. She was within walking distance of the magnificent Shibden Hall, and almost certainly spent time there and drew inspiration from it for her image of Thrushcross Grange in Wuthering Heights.

Branwell

Talented in music, art and writing, Branwell was not to live up to his family's expectations. Ill-equipped for life, he gave way to alcohol and drugs and died tragically.

rage, she accused Charlotte of betrayal and having destroyed the one thing that meant so much to her: the secret, private world of her innermost thoughts and feelings. But somehow, with Anne's assistance, the storm abated, Emily eventually consenting to Charlotte's proposal that the three of them each contribute some of their poems for a joint volume of verse.

Although *Poems by Currer, Ellis and Acton Bell* failed commercially, the three sisters each embarked on the writing of a novel. Writing under her nom-de-plume of 'Ellis Bell', Emily wrote *Wuthering Heights* between the autumn of 1845 and her 28th birthday in July 1846. It met with a favourable public response, though the literary establishment condemned it variously as 'disgusting', 'inhuman', 'evil', 'uncivilized', 'artistically immature'. To Emily, their response was entirely predictable and of little consequence.

Within a year of the publication of *Wuthering Heights* Branwell was dead, succumbing to the ravages of consumption, alcohol and drugs. At his funeral in October 1848 Emily caught a cold. Suffering from pains in the chest, shortness of breath and a hacking cough, she nevertheless refused to rest, take medicine or permit the attendance of a doctor. Painfully thin and white, she continued to perform her daily tasks – rising at seven in the morning, feeding her animals, returning to her cold bed at ten o'clock at night.

On the morning of 19 December when she rose as usual at seven, the death-rattle could be heard distinctly as she dragged herself downstairs. Charlotte gave her a last sprig of heather gathered from the moor. She was too far gone to recognize it. Lying on the horsehair sofa in the sitting-room, she made a last concession to her sisters. 'If you'll send for a doctor I'll see him now', she whispered, dying moments later. She was buried at Haworth Church on 22 December. Keeper, her devoted dog, howled outside her bedroom door for weeks after her departure.

Charlotte Brontë
(left) Emily did not have an easy relationship with her elder sister. But whatever their differences, Charlotte never failed to be impressed by her sister's strength of will and sharp, penetrating mind.

Sir Walter Scott
(right) Charlotte wrote to a friend 'For fiction, read Scott alone; all novels after him are worthless.' And a young Emily named him as one of the three men she would wish to be with her on a dream island. His novels presented to her a prototype of ideal womanhood – independent and daring, and scornful of lesser minds. That was how she envisioned her heroines, and how she herself wished to be.

WUTHERING HEIGHTS

The windswept desolation of the Yorkshire Moors frames the tempestuous passions of Cathy and Heathcliff. The story of their tortured love achieves a unique emotional intensity.

Since its publication in 1847, *Wuthering Heights* has become one of the most admired and popular of all English novels. Its single-minded intensity, forcefulness of expression, and haunting, sombre themes have captured the imagination of millions. The world with which it deals is at once vividly physical and intensely spiritual. Central to the drama stand Heathcliff and Cathy, whose passion has become almost a byword for the height of romantic love.

GUIDE TO THE PLOT

The story is told by two narrators, and moves from the Yorkshire of 1801, back 25 years to encompass the plot. It opens with a diary entry of Mr Lockwood, a foppish southerner, who has withdrawn from the world for a while, and taken up tenancy of Thrushcross Grange on the wild Yorkshire moors. He visits his landlord, Mr Heathcliff at his isolated farmhouse, Wuthering Heights, where he receives a decidedly hostile reception. But Lockwood is intrigued by his dark, morose landlord, and makes a second visit.

Forced to stay the night because of a storm, Lockwood experiences a vivid and violent nightmare. He dreams that he puts his hand out of the window to silence the tapping of a tree-branch on the pane. But his "fingers closed on the fingers of a little, ice-cold hand!". A melancholy voice wails "Let me in!", and the vision of a child – calling herself Catherine Linton – tells him she has been a waif for 20 years. In his horror, to get loose from the child's grasp he slashes her wrist against the broken glass. Heathcliff is woken by the commotion, and on discovering Lockwood's 'dream' breaks down in a "passion of grief", and begs the waif, Cathy, to come back to him.

Lockwood's return to the Grange in deep

Foppish narrator
Heathcliff's tenant, Mr Lockwood is an outsider from the city. Prevented from returning to Thrushcross Grange because of a snow storm, he seeks shelter at Wuthering Heights – his "nightmare vision" of Cathy's ghost throws the story into motion.

Savage landscape
Cathy and Heathcliff's passion is as savage and elemental as the landscape that is their spiritual home. Their relationship is set among the rocky crags, ravaged by stormy elements, away from "the stir of society" and the norms of civilized behaviour.

snow brings on a fever, and to while away his convalescence, he asks the housekeeper, Ellen (Nelly) Dean, to tell him what she knows of Heathcliff and his household. Ellen, who has spent her life in service between the bleak Wuthering Heights, and the more comfortable and elegant Thrushcross Grange, obligingly settles down to tell him the story.

Ellen's first memories are of being at Wuthering Heights as a girl, when her master, old Mr Earnshaw returns home from a journey from Liverpool with a "dirty, ragged black-haired child" whom he has found starving in the streets. The foundling, "as dark almost as if it came from the devil", is named simply Heathcliff. Earnshaw's son and heir Hindley hates the boy, but his daughter Cathy becomes "very thick" with him. As the years pass, and with Hindley away at school, Cathy and Heathcliff become almost inseparable.

When old Mr Earnshaw dies, Hindley returns as master, along with his sickly wife. Hindley treats the adolescent Heathcliff in a callous and degrading way, relegating him to the position of a labourer and flogging him frequently. In spite of this treatment, the bond between Heathcliff and Cathy grows. Their spiritual unity is characterized by their shared passion for the wild moors.

One night, while wandering in the grounds of nearby Thrushcross Grange, Cathy is bitten by a guard dog and stays at the Grange to recover. She befriends the children of the house, Edgar and Isabella Linton, and is introduced to a civilized life of comfort and manners.

Hindley's wife dies shortly after giving birth to a son, Hareton, and Hindley takes

refuge in drunkenness, violence and gambling. His increasing tyranny rouses Heathcliff's implacable hatred and desire for revenge. Meanwhile, Edgar's admiration for Cathy turns to love and she is confronted with a choice between him and Heathcliff.

The lure of worldly advantages attracts her and she declares to Nelly her intention of accepting Edgar, even though by doing so she is betraying her own soul. "It would degrade me to marry Heathcliff, now . . ." she cries. Heathcliff overhears, and that night, during a furious storm, disappears.

In spite of Cathy's grief over the loss of her soulmate, she continues to see Edgar and three years later the couple marry. Leaving Hareton to the care of his increasingly degenerate father, Nelly leaves the Heights to join Cathy at Thrushcross Grange.

> " 'My love for Linton is like the foliage in the woods. Time will change it... as winter changes the trees – my love for Heathcliff resembles the eternal rocks beneath – a source of little visible delight, but necessary. Nelly, I am Heathcliff – he's always, always in my mind' "

Childhood rivals
(above) When old Mr Earnshaw brings home the foundling Heathcliff, his son Hindley immediately detests the "dirty, ragged, black-haired child". Nelly Dean, the second narrator, tells how Heathcliff "would stand Hindley's blows without winking or shedding a tear". But Heathcliff is determined to wreak revenge.

Thrushcross Grange
(left) The Lintons introduce Cathy to an elegant life at Thrushcross Grange. Refined and genteel, they regard Heathcliff as "worse than a brute" and influence Cathy's opinion of him. When Edgar Linton begins to court her, she has to choose between them.

The peaceful existence of the Grange is irrevocably shattered by the sudden return of Heathcliff, who has grown into a tall, imposing man and acquired education and wealth by mysterious means. He now looks like a gentleman – but a "half-civilized ferocity lurked yet in the depressed brows and eyes full of black fire". He exploits Hindley's spiralling degeneracy, and encourages Isabella Linton's infatuation for him.

Heathcliff's mysterious return and altered appearance rekindles more intensely than before the passion between him and Cathy, but now their relationship is marked by mutual recrimination and tortured need. After a single passionate encounter, Heathcliff loses Cathy; but remains haunted by her presence. His only reality becomes his driving obsession with thwarting the lives of the Earnshaws and the Lintons – the lengths to which he goes reveal him both as the tormented and the tormentor. Only at the end does a resolution – of sorts – come about.

TRAGIC ROMANCE

The immense power and originality of *Wuthering Heights* is undeniable, but precisely how to define the novel is less simple. At its heart lies the relationship between Cathy and Heathcliff, but to term it a mere love story would not encompass its breathtaking force. In charting the roots of

passion, the betrayal of that passion by Cathy and the consequences of her betrayal, *Wuthering Heights* can best be described as a romantic tragedy. Its haunting themes are simultaneously harsh and brooding, and are captured by a poetic imagination.

Cathy and Heathcliff provide much of the book's emotional force, but the impact of the relationship is made more startling by its setting: their heights and depths of emotion are defined against a backdrop of humdrum everyday living.

The world of *Wuthering Heights* is essentially one of contrasts. It is a world in which pain and beauty exist side by side: untrammelled passion is set against the conventional, regulated love of Edgar Linton; the natural laws which govern Cathy and Heathcliff contrast with the pious cant of old Joseph or the social moralising of Nelly.

Part of the novel's ageless appeal is due to the forceful directness of the language. Free from any conscious style or apparent intrusion by the author, the story is expressed simply and plainly, with informal and largely colloquial dialogue. There are frequent glimpses of Emily's poetic gifts. In passages describing the love between Cathy and Heathcliff the writing achieves the lyrical beauty and cadence of poetry:

'I dreamt I was sleeping the last sleep, by that sleeper, with my heart stopped, and my cheek frozen against hers.'

Fierce passions
After several years' absence, Heathcliff returns to Wuthering Heights – "a tall, athletic, well-framed man . . . his manner was even dignified . . . though too stern for grace" with a fortune and a compelling force of character – and the love between him and Cathy is rekindled, even more fiercely than before. Their violent passion is only once consummated before Cathy dies. Heathcliff's obsession with his dead love finally brings them together, but not before he has carried out a terrible vengeance.

G. Courbet: The Lovers (Detail)/Musee des Beaux Arts, Lyon. Giraudon

---

In the Background

GYPSIES, WAIFS AND STRAYS

Yorkshire folklore invested travelling gypsy bands with inhuman qualities. A popular belief was that they were waifs or 'waffs' – apparitions prophesying death. Hell-fire Methodists, like Emily's Aunt Branwell, helped spread the suspicions. Heathcliff's origins remain mysterious, but he is perceived as a "gypsy brat" that is "as dark almost as if it came from the devil". And he is named after Earnshaw's son who died in childbirth.

Gypsies
Travelling bands roamed the length of the Pennines, and became a part of the lurid folklore of the surrounding area.

F. Walker, The Vagrants (Detail)/Tate Gallery, London

The attachment between Heathcliff and Cathy can hardly be described as affection – it is a soaring, consuming, profound *need*, which in being denied fulfilment becomes selfish and destructive. Their emotion is felt at such a pitch that it transcends the demands and conventions of ordinary life. Judged on its own, Edgar's love for Cathy might seem a strong feeling, but set against Heathcliff's larger passion it is "paltry" and "insipid".

> " *'I was wild after she died, and eternally, from dawn to dawn, praying her to return to me – her spirit – I have a strong faith in ghosts; I have a conviction that they can, and do exist, among us!'* "

Emily Brontë is concerned less with the individual emotions of her hero and heroine than with their mutual despair at the limitations of the world and their struggle to break through those confines. In Cathy, but even more in the enigmatic and relentless Heathcliff, Emily Brontë exposes basic human drives with none of the shams and cloaks of civilization. The characters act like the natural

Solid Yorkshire
(left) Domestic life at Wuthering Heights is basic and elemental: "the house and kitchen . . .with great fires" looks like a typical north country farmhouse. The mundane, homely setting throws into relief the extraordinary experiences of its inhabitants.

Cruel treatment
(above) Both Hindley and Heathcliff become degenerate tyrants capable of extreme cruelty. After Cathy's death, Heathcliff seems bent on corrupting all those connected with the Lintons. Hindley's son Hareton is only just saved from a similar cruel fate.

The second generation
At first, the children of original characters seem to show history repeating itself. Little Hareton (above) is brought up to be sullen and coarse as Heathcliff once was. And Cathy's proud daughter Catherine thinks that he is not good enough for her. But gradually, a real and enduring love grows between them.

forces they feel so akin to. Their real home is neither Wuthering Heights or Thrushcross Grange, but the wild, craggy moors.

Although the relationship is described with little outward physicality, its effect is of extreme physical and sexual force as well as spiritual intensity. Cathy and Heathcliff are incomplete as separate beings; their identity is provided by the other. As an adolescent, Cathy declares dramatically: "Nelly, I *am* Heathcliff", while Heathcliff himself is left in a state of torment by Cathy's death because of this bond: "I cannot live without my soul!" he cries. And his only real desire is for a union with her beyond the grave.

MYSTERIOUS HEATHCLIFF

For all her wildness, Cathy is firmly rooted in the human sphere. But in creating Heathcliff, Emily Brontë provides no parallel base. His beginnings are mysterious, his movements cloaked in mystery. Isabella Linton's puzzled questions may be echoed by readers when she asks, "Is Mr Heathcliff a man? If so, is he mad? And if not, is he a devil?" But just as Isabella finds him an irresistible figure, despite his savage and cruel nature, so have generations of readers.

Heathcliff embodies all Emily Brontë's brooding, Romantic imagination – he is dangerous and fiendish, but he is also charismatic and passionate. He is a kind of devil, "an evil beast . . . waiting his time to spring and destroy", and as such Emily Brontë invites the reader to condemn him. But by showing him as a child – abandoned, saved only to be abandoned again, ill-treated and humiliated, yet proud and intensely loyal to Cathy, he arouses our sympathy.

Through him, Emily Brontë reveals her own scorn of easy moralising. When Heathcliff sits brooding on how to get his revenge on Hindley, Nelly's rebuke, "For shame, Heathcliff! . . . It is for God to punish wicked people; we should learn to forgive" seems a mere nod to convention. It is less persuasive than Heathcliff's honest retort: "No, God won't have the satisfaction that I shall."

Wuthering Heights is, as Emily's sister Charlotte described it, 'hewn in a wild workshop' – the product of an intensely personal and uncompromising vision. Emily Brontë's genius lay in involving the reader in a timeless and poetic world. At the end of the novel, when a frightened little Yorkshire lad claims to have seen the ghosts of Heathcliff and Cathy near Wuthering Heights: "They's Heathcliff and a woman, yonder, under t'Nab . . . un' Aw darnut pass 'em", like Nelly we cannot help but half believe him.

CHARACTERS IN FOCUS

Part of the enormous power of *Wuthering Heights* arises from the extreme contrasts between its characters. The dark, tempestuous Earnshaws and the even darker and more intense Heathcliff inhabit a completely different world from that of the fair, refined Edgar and Isabella Linton. The sensible narrator Nelly Dean, and the grumpy old servant Joseph provide a streak of Yorkshire hard-headedness.

Hindley Earnshaw's lifelong hatred for Heathcliff begins when old Mr Earnshaw 'adopts' him. As a youth, Hindley torments Heathcliff, and when he becomes master of Wuthering Heights, he degrades and punishes him. But after his wife's death, Hindley "grew desperate . . . and gave himself up to reckless dissipation", and Heathcliff is only too ready to take advantage of his degeneracy and complete his descent into drunkenness and ruin.

WHO'S WHO

Cathy Earnshaw A "wild, wicked slip" with the "bonniest eye and sweetest smile". Passionate and headstrong, she chooses between Edgar and Heathcliff with fateful results.

Heathcliff A foundling, brought to Wuthering Heights by old Mr Earnshaw. He grows up to be a handsome, "fierce, pitiless, wolfish man", consumed by his attachment to Cathy.

Hindley Earnshaw Cathy's brother, and master of Wuthering Heights after their father's death. He despises and degrades Heathcliff.

Mr Lockwood Mr Heathcliff's tenant. An idle, foppish citydweller. His diary entry starts the story.

Ellen (Nelly) Dean Housekeeper in her time of both Wuthering Heights and Thrushcross Grange. She relates the story to Lockwood.

Edgar Linton Mild, fair-headed and refined, he becomes the master of Thrushcross Grange, and marries Cathy.

Isabella Linton Edgar's younger sister. Brought up in comfort and ease, Isabella becomes infatuated with Heathcliff.

Hareton Earnshaw Hindley's son. Proud and warm by nature, he is brought up by Hindley and Heathcliff to be coarse and brutish.

Catherine Linton Daughter of Cathy and Edgar. Heathcliff manipulates her into marrying Linton.

Linton Heathcliff The sickly, complaining, cruel son of Heathcliff and Isabella. "A pale, delicate, effeminate boy".

Joseph The fanatical, judgemental old servant at Wuthering Heights.

"A haughty, headstrong creature, passionate and wilful", Cathy (right) is caught between the two worlds of Heathcliff and Edgar – the one intense, unconventional and allied to the natural extremes of the windswept moors, the other affectionate, respectable, refined, but insipid. She "betrays her own heart" by choosing to marry Edgar rather than her soulmate, and pays for it with her death. Essentially childlike and capricious, Cathy in her troubled womanhood yearns for the childhood happiness she knew with Heathcliff: "I wish I were out of doors – I wish I were a girl again, half savage and hardy, and free".

"A charming young lady of eighteen; infantile in manners" Isabella Linton (below) is irresistibly attracted to Heathcliff and infatuated by her own romantic idea of him. Despite Cathy's warnings – "he'd crush you, like a sparrow's egg" – and Heathcliff's own deliberately cruel behaviour, she elopes with him. Once married and living an isolated, brutal existence at Wuthering Heights, she realizes her mistake, and escapes – to give birth to his weakling son, Linton.

The family servant at Wuthering Heights, Joseph is the "wearisomest, self-righteous pharisee that ever ransacked a Bible". He is always ready to deliver some religious cant in his broad Yorkshire dialect. Although he stays on when Heathcliff is owner of Wuthering Heights, he is overjoyed at Heathcliff's death: "Th' divil's harried off his soul . . . and he muh hev his carcass intuh the bargain, for owt Aw care!" he cries, before kneeling to pray.

W.H. Hunt: the Faithful Old Servant. (Detail) Victoria and Albert Museum; Bridgeman Art Library

Heathcliff's brooding presence is the most powerful force in the novel. Dark and mysterious, with "brows lowering, the eyes deep set and singular", he is first introduced as a morose, reclusive man – "a dark-skinned gypsy in aspect, in dress and manners a gentleman". As Nelly relates his story to Mr Lockwood, we learn that he was discovered starving in the streets of Liverpool, and brought home by Cathy's father to Wuthering Heights. As children, he and Cathy share a delight in the freedom of Nature, but other characters endow him with supernatural characteristics – he is described throughout as a fiend and a demon. Relentless and sadistic in his treatment of everyone except Cathy, his life becomes hell when she is separated from him by her death. His tortured pursuit of her ghost finally achieves a strange, savage fulfilment.

"I certainly esteem myself a steady, reasonable sort of body" Nelly Dean tells Mr Lockwood as she relates the strange story of Cathy and Heathcliff. She has been in service to the Earnshaws and Lintons at both Wuthering Heights and Thrushcross Grange ever since she was a child, and was witness to all the events. Hers is the voice of homely wisdom, and conventional morality. As a young woman she was always on hand to give both Heathcliff and Cathy advice, and she remains in her background, supportive role throughout the story. But at the end, having heard stories of the ghosts of Cathy and Heathcliff walking together, she tells Lockwood how she half believes them. "I don't like being out in the dark now; and I don't like being left by myself in this grim house . . . I shall be glad when they leave it, and shift to the Grange."

W. Mulready: Interior with a Portrait of John Sheepshanks. (Detail) Victoria and Albert Museum

F. D. Hardy: The Young Photographers. (Detail) Christies, Bridgeman Art Library

Edgar Linton is the opposite of Heathcliff both in looks and temperament. With his "soft-featured face . . . pensive, amiable expression . . . the eyes were large and serious, the figure almost too graceful", he "wanted spirit in general". He loves Cathy deeply, but his emotions cannot match hers in intensity. To Cathy and Heathcliff his lack of passion means that he is weak: Cathy says that his veins are "full of ice-water", while Heathcliff calls him a "milk-blooded coward".

WOMEN OF VISION

From childhood, Emily and Anne Brontë shared an imaginary world which gave them mutual solace and inspiration, and nourished their extraordinary adult writings.

Soon after the death of her beloved sister Emily, Anne Brontë wrote:

> O Thou has taken my delight
> And hope of life away!

Emily had been Anne's one true soulmate and companion. 'Emily . . . and Anne were like twins – inseparable companions', recalled Charlotte's friend Ellen Nussey after their deaths. Both were shy and withdrawn, and their profound love of Haworth Moor gave them not only emotional and spiritual succour, but also poetic inspiration. And from an early age they were both deeply involved in the fantasy world of Gondal – their first, since lost, literary work.

THE GONDAL WORLD

Emily was 12½ and Anne 11 when they created Gondal. It was to prove much more than child's play, and continue long into adulthood. It became a secret world which they alone shared, enabling them to express their feelings to each other without surrendering their natural reticence or privacy. Gondal was not remotely like the world most young girls might construct around their dolls. It was a kingdom, almost always in a state of crisis, stricken by armed rebellion, republican uprisings, invasion, treason, treachery and murder. The violence of the place, and the passions

expressed by the Gondal characters, anticipated the novels of both girls.

The names they gave their characters were a marvel of invention: exotic, romantic, extravagant. In one of her diary papers dated 30 July 1845, her 27th birthday, Emily wrote of an excursion she and Anne had taken to York in June of that year (Emily and Anne wrote notes to each other on their birthdays, to be opened four years later). There is little about the visit itself, but she notes that:

'during our excursion we were, Ronald Macalgin, Henry Angora . . . Julian Egremont, Catherine Navarre, and Cordelia Fitzaphnold, escaping from the palaces of instruction to join the Royalists who are hard driven at present by the victorious Republicans. The Gondals still flourish as bright as ever. We intend sticking firm by the rascals as long as they delight us . . .'

Gondal provided both girls with a fictional realm in which they could exercise their vivid imaginations, to the extent that, as Emily suggests, they 'were' or they 'became' their creations. It also enabled them, through their (often male) characters, to think and act vicariously in ways denied them as the daughters of a widowed clergyman living in a remote Yorkshire parsonage – a home with a peculiarly bleak outlook over a graveyard on one

C. Holsoe: Girl Reading in an Interior/Gavin Graham Gallery, Bridgeman Art Library

The germ of inspiration
Emily and Anne collaborated with their brother and sister in their earliest imaginative work, Glasstown. *It was partly inspired by the grand Biblical pictures (left) at the parsonage.*

side and the windswept moors on the other. The imaginary world of the Gondals was, in fact, far more like the 'real' world than the two young ladies from the parsonage could possibly have known.

Under these assumed identities, but also in her own voice, Emily wrote poetry of a very high order. Using a simple ballad form, she speaks of her chosen isolation from a world whose riches mean nothing to her, and of her longing for a freedom which ultimately, she realizes, only death can bring:

> Riches I hold in light esteem
> And Love I laugh to scorn
> And lust of Fame was but a dream
> That vanished with the morn –

J. Martin: Jacob's Dream/Christies. Bridgeman Art Library

And if I pray, the only prayer
That moves my lips for me
Is – 'Leave the heart that now I bear
And give me liberty.'

Death is not the end of life, but the birth of the life of the soul, which, freed from the shackles of the body, rises "beyond and above". In moments of quietness, alone on the moor under the burning sun, Emily Brontë experienced moments of visionary insight, later captured in the best of her poems. At such moments she felt that the unseen world of the soul had a reality greater than that perceived by the five senses.

Like Cathy in *Wuthering Heights*, Emily's only declared fear is that death may mean total separation from the Earth:

We would not leave our native home
For any world beyond the tomb.

Also like her heroine, Emily does not yearn for a conventional Christian Heaven, but for oneness with the Universe – one with the wind and the rain, the sunlight and the stars. Nature, never sentimentalized, rarely benign, is contrasted with the fretfulness of human existence:

How beautiful the Earth is still
. . . – how full of Happiness;
How little fraught with real ill
Or shadowy phantoms of distress;

To all outward appearances Emily Brontë lived a life of little joy. Isolated, friendless, loved by none but her family and sorely grieved by Branwell's physical and mental degeneration, she nevertheless found delight and comfort in the rich world of her own imagination. In *To Imagination* (1844), she writes of the two worlds she is forced to inhabit and of the greater hope and solace of the invisible world:

The world where guile and hate and doubt
And cold suspicion never rise;
Where thou and I and Liberty
Have undisputed sovereignty.

Ambivalent pseudonyms
(left) Like Charlotte, Emily and Anne published their work under androgynous pseudonyms – an indication of their aversion to publicity and desire to be judged impartially.

A solitary spirit
(left) The glorious 'inner world' of freedom which Emily created in her poetry transcended the tedium, paltriness and convention so irksome to her in the everyday life she was forced to live.

Childhood reading
From *The Arabian Nights* (above) the Brontës 'lifted' the idea of genii. Each child was both the guardian and creator of a favourite character, and was invested with magic powers.

Tales of violence
(right) Clashes at political and religious gatherings were not uncommon during the Brontës' formative years. Stories of these outbreaks was one of the many early influences on Emily.

Gondal poetry
(left) The surviving manuscripts of the Gondal saga are of poems written for its characters, but expressing their authors' private sentiments. It was only with difficulty that Emily was persuaded to publish them.

The Gondals' home
(below) Gondal was a fictional island kingdom in the North Pacific, half-real, half-fantasy in its landscape of splendid lakes and heath-covered mountains in which the Gondals' heroic exploits were played out.

Anne Brontë's view of poetry is expressed in her semi-autobiographical novel, *Agnes Grey*. "When we are harassed", she writes, "by sorrows or anxieties, or long oppressed by any powerful feelings which we must keep to ourselves, for which we can obtain and seek no sympathy from any living creature . . . we often naturally seek relief in poetry . . .".

A LOVE OF FREEDOM

For Anne poetry is not a means of revelation – as it is for Emily – but a source of "relief". Nostalgia for a better place or a better time is a common theme. Already at the age of 16 she looks back to the days when

> . . . long ago I loved to lie
> Upon the pathless moor,
> To hear the wild wind rushing by
> With never ceasing roar;

Perhaps the happiest days of Anne's life were spent roaming free over the moors with Emily before school darkened their existence. "Oh, happy life!" she sings in another early poem, "To range the mountains wild". They were carefree days as she recalls them, a time when, "I loved the free and open sky/ Better than books and tutors grim".

Of Anne's 59 surviving poems, 16 of them are signed by Gondal characters, many by Anne's two chief protagonists, 'Alexandrina Zenobia' and her lover, 'Alexander Hybernia'. These poems are dramatic, full of powerful sentiments and forceful expressions. They show a boldness and love of freedom which she shares with Emily, and which make her appear more interesting than Charlotte's description of her 'sensitive, reserved and dejected nature' suggests. Outlaws, fugitive lovers and brave and daring young men are favourite personae of Anne's:

> I was roaming light and gay
> Upon a breezy summer day,
> A bold and careless youth . . .

– and in this world "Danger and freedom both were there!"

In 1846, Anne, Emily and Charlotte published a collection of *Poems*. Anne contributed 21 poems to this edition, almost all of a personal nature and of recent composition. Though perhaps not technically perfect, their simple rhythms reflect a sincere, reflective mind, saddened by the recent death of her beloved, William Weightman:

> Yes, thou art gone! and never more
> Thy sunny smile shall gladden me . . .

These lyrics of lament gave no indication of the worldly insight Anne put into her two novels. *Agnes Grey* was based on Anne's painful experiences as a governess with the Ingham family. For the accuracy with which she depicted the snobbishness of her employers and the viciousness of her charges, she was accused 'of extravagant over-colouring'. But the physically frail Anne was undaunted by the voice of outraged Victorian hypocrisy,

44

Childhood rambles

(left) The greatest single influence on both Anne and Emily was their native moors, ravines and brooks. Rambling out in fine weather they would admire 'every moss, every flower, every tint and form' in which 'Emily especially had a gleesome delight'. Here they experienced true freedom, and their first writings were nurtured here.

and in her Preface to *The Tenant of Wildfell Hall*, her second novel, she defends the absolute necessity of telling the truth – '. . . if there were less of this delicate concealment of facts . . . there would be less of sin and misery to the young of both sexes who are left to wring their bitter knowledge from experience'.

The immediate impetus for this novel was to be found in Branwell's final decline. Joining Anne at Thorp Green Hall to work for the Robinson family, he courted the dazzling and unscrupulous Mrs Robinson, believing that she returned his passion. The disastrous 'affair' marked the beginning of the end for Branwell, and Anne felt herself responsible for this and her family's consequent suffering.

Acutely aware of Branwell's and her own lack of education in the ways of the world,

Simon Warner

Ponden Hall

(left) Three miles from Haworth, the grand home of the Heaton family inspired the creation of Emily's Thrushcross Grange and Anne's Wildfell Hall. Both writers were able to transform the places they knew well into potent images in which their powerful, tormented figures enact their dramas.

she set about warning others. Through the dissolute characters of Arthur Huntingdon and his fashionable set she exposes the fatal and corrupting effects of self-indulgence. And in the person of her heroine, Helen Huntingdon, she makes a powerful vindication of a woman's dignity within marriage.

But *The Tenant of Wildfell Hall* is no self-righteous diatribe. Honest as well as original, the 'good' characters are not straightforward paragons of virtue. Helen herself is dangerously indulgent of her future husband's faults, and over-confident of her ability to reform him. And Gilbert Markham, who falls deeply in love with her, is prone both to outbursts of spiteful anger, and to comical lapses into priggishness.

Published in June 1848, the novel was an overnight success. Critics condemned it for 'a morbid love of the coarse, if not the brutal', but its popularity with the general public may have been for this very reason. Few were to know that the stamp of the author's brother was on every page, or the effort it caused her – sitting 'bent over her desk' – to write it.

The physical and emotional rigours of Anne's life at last took their toll. Like Emily, she had long had a premonition of early death and in her calm, stoical way, welcomed its release:

> There is a rest beyond the grave,
> A lasting rest from pain and sin . . .
> Show me that rest – I ask no more.

On 28 May 1849, five months after Emily's death, Anne Brontë's final wish was granted.

A severe lesson

(right) In The Tenant of Wildfell Hall, *Anne put her bitter experience as a governess to positive use. But her main intention was to expose the evils of a debauched way of life, and to protect the young who were made particularly vulnerable by society's tacit sanction of immoral, but fashionable behaviour.*

R.B. Martineau: The Last Day in the Old Home (Detail/Tate Gallery, London

Uniquely talented but tragically ill-fated, the Brontë sisters wrote some of the most passionate fiction ever penned. Chiefly remembered for her magnificent *Wuthering Heights*, Emily was also the author of intense and moving poetry, while her gentle sister Anne wrote two novels that shocked and excited the reading public when first published. The quality of their work owes much to their sisterhood. Despite the brevity of their own remarkably uneventful lives, they were far from overshadowed by their more famous sister Charlotte. Their work is charged with an emotional intensity that is both startling and powerful, and their themes and characters accurately reflect the background and the tragedy against which they wrote – they witnessed the mental anguish and physical disintegration of their brother Branwell, and seemed to have a premonition of their own untimely deaths.

H. Jutsum: The River Nidd near Knaresborough, Yorks/Fine Art Photographic Library

POEMS
by Emily Brontë

+ 1846 +

Emily Brontë would have been assured of a place in English literature had she never written *Wuthering Heights*. On discovering Emily's poetry, Charlotte instinctively responded to its unique beauty, describing it as 'wild, melancholy and elevating'. Its intensity of emotional expression reveals Emily's feeling for suffering humanity, and her Gondal poem "Cold in the earth" has been called 'one of the greatest poems . . . in the language'. Emily contributed 22 of the *Poems* by Currer, Ellis and Acton Bell, first published in 1846, but it was only after her death that the real value of her work was recognized. The Victorian critic and poet Matthew Arnold compared her with Byron, saying that she was someone "whose soul/Knew no fellow for might,/Passion, vehemence, grief,/Daring, since Byron died". G. K. Chesterton, writing a generation later, saw in Emily's poetry 'elemental emotion' and a 'nature-worship such as has often been the religion of . . . proud and unhappy human beings'. It was not until 1941 that the *Complete Poems* – 193 in all – edited by C. W. Hatfield, was finally published. Her biographer, Winifred Gérin, has said that many more poems by Emily and Anne were destroyed by Charlotte after their deaths. Anne's talent as a poet was certainly a lesser one than her sister's, but was justly described as sincere. Almost half of the 54 remaining are on Gondal themes, while five commemorate her love for William Weightman, her father's curate, whose death in 1842 she mourned for the rest of her life.

Edimedia

THE TENANT OF WILDFELL HALL
by Anne Brontë
→ 1848 ←

Helen Graham, pictured below with her son, is the mysterious *Tenant of Wildfell Hall*. Anne Brontë relates her story in three parts. The first, narrated by Gilbert Markham, tells of his meeting with the beautiful Helen and his love for her. Enigmatically, she rejects his advances, offering him her diary to read as an explanation.

The diary fills in the background: Helen is the runaway wife of Arthur Huntingdon (inset). His world is one of debauchery, his chief amusements are getting drunk and making love to other men's wives. Worried about his corrupting influence on her son, she flees.

The final section tells of Huntingdon's sorry end and Helen's marriage to Markham. The novel was a success and the author's identity a subject of much debate. People argued that such bold language and sexually explicit scenes could not have been penned by a woman, but then Anne Brontë was certainly no ordinary woman.

AGNES GREY
by Anne Brontë
→ 1847 ←

Agnes Grey (above, inset) becomes a governess to help her impoverished family, little realizing the humiliations in store. Her first charges behave abominably. Their planned persecution of Agnes becomes almost sinister, but she bears it with fortitude, only to be unfairly dismissed.

The book is largely autobiographical. The plight of the Victorian governess was one Anne Brontë experienced, first at Blake Hall, then at Thorp Green which, in *Agnes Grey*, becomes the country house of the Murrays. 'Educating' the unruly Murray teenagers proves almost impossible. They and their parents lack all moral sense. Agnes is sustained only by her love for Edmund Weston, the local curate. Before their love can be expressed, however, Agnes is obliged to leave and open a seaside school with her mother. Here Mr Weston seeks her out and courts her.

The novel begins by saying, "All true histories contain instruction". In her aim to instruct, Anne certainly succeeded, for in 1868 Lady Amberley noted in her diary, 'read *Agnes Grey* . . . should like to give it to every family with a governess and shall read it through again when I have a governess, to remind me to be human'.

Yorkshire Life

The steely strengths of Yorkshire character were put to the test by the Industrial Revolution. It starved and subjugated the majority, but created a new breed of Yorkshireman: the self-made capitalist.

The pale, tough grass and dun heather, the tumbling becks and black rock of the wild, windswept moors around Haworth are as much a part of *Wuthering Heights* as Cathy and Heathcliff themselves. Yet Emily Brontë drew her inspiration not only from the fells and dales of Yorkshire, but also from the hardy, proud breed of people who lived among them.

Emily rarely left the Parsonage in Haworth except to go to church or stride out alone across the moors, and had little direct contact with local people. And yet, according to her sister Charlotte, 'she knew them: knew their ways, their language, their family histories; she could hear of them with interest, and talk of them with detail, minute, graphic, and accurate'.

The pages of *Wuthering Heights* are filled with echoes of the distinctive character of Yorkshire folk, their rugged independence contrasting with the bland softness of 'offcomers' like the narrator Mr Lockwood. Indeed, Emily may have found the basic idea for the plot locally, in the sad story of the Walkers, a Halifax family of farmers and manufacturers, whose fortunes were bedevilled by an adopted son.

PROUD CRAFTSMEN

At the time Emily Brontë was writing, the distinctive Yorkshire character was already a byword: dour and pragmatic, cautious but blunt, suspicious of strangers yet warm-hearted and proudly independent – a character moulded by centuries of wresting a living from a harsh landscape, often on remote hill farms. But the three decades of Emily's life saw Yorkshire and Yorkshire lives changing dramatically as the Industrial Revolution stormed through the West Riding.

Perched high on the bleak moors, Haworth seems far removed from the great centres of industry today. Yet it was not so when the Brontës first went to live there in 1820. Haworth was not a remote farming community then, but one of a dense cluster of bustling manufacturing villages that ran all the way down the steep valleys of the Aire and Calder to Bradford and Halifax. In the solid, grey stone cottages of these villages worked thousands of independent master clothiers – 'little makers' – and weavers and woolcombers who had helped make the West Riding of Yorkshire the focus of the English fine woollen and worsted industry. The wool came from Yorkshire sheep.

It was the small master clothiers, more than anyone, who created the Yorkshire reputation for bluntness and bluff pride – their way of life fostered a sense of independence. Half a century previously, the small master clothier would ride over to the Yorkshire Wolds to buy his own raw wool. He would weave the wool himself on a hand-loom, perhaps employing a few journeyman weavers to help him, and then ride over to Halifax or Leeds to sell the cloth independently in the great Cloth Hall. By 1800, he had come to rely on merchants to buy and sell wool, but he was still free to work as and when he pleased.

Writing of Cleckheaton in the 1830s, Frank Peel described the character of the small master clothier:

P. Reinagle: The Afternoon Shoot/Roy Miles Gallery/Bridgeman Art Library

Hunting with gundogs
(above) Hunting and shooting were the prime leisure pursuits of the gentleman farmer, the rugged landscapes providing excellent sport.

P. Serusier: The Weaver/Musée du Hauberger, Senlis/Bridgeman Art Library

The cottage weaver
(left) Weavers had a secure, if limited, income and a proud independence – until the mills opened and made craftsmanship defunct almost overnight.

'dark, satanic mills'
(left) Yorkshire became the
centre of the textile world.
Some mill-owners adopted a
fatherly role, providing
schooling, housing and
health care for their workers.
For the majority, however,
work in the mills meant
squalor, malnutrition and an
early death.

The Victorian family
(below) The traditional
image of the large Victorian
family was a reality, but
only the children of the
well-to-do (most of whom
belonged to a new class) had
a better-than-even chance of
surviving infancy.

God's estate
A strict and austere piety
governed all aspects of
Yorkshire life. The
Methodist movement thrived
in town and country,
encouraging thrift, hard
work and suspicions as
deep-rooted as the colourful
folklore.

'The little makers were men who doffed their caps to
no one, and recognized no right in either squire or
parson to question, or meddle with them . . . Their
brusqueness and plain speaking might at times be of-
fensive . . . If the little maker rose in the world high
enough to employ a few of his neighbours, he did not
therefore cease to labour with his own hands, but
worked as hard or perhaps harder than anyone he
employed. In speech and in dress he claimed no
superiority'. An admirable race.

Towards the end of the 18th century, with demand
for fine woollens rising and prices high, woolcombers
and croppers, and even journeyman weavers, earned
a good enough income to infect them with a similar
sense of independence – good enough for them to
barely notice the loss of control over their lives.

49

Robbed of their trade, and indeed of any work, the woolcraftsmen of Haworth and the other villages of the West Riding sank into terrible poverty. Shrugging off their traditional pride, they trekked into Bradford and Leeds to beg for work in the factories. There they met with thousands of other destitute migrants, from the Yorkshire countryside and beyond, forced off the land by the enclosure movement (in the interests of more efficient farming techniques). To Bradford in the 1820s, 'they came from Kendal, North Yorkshire, Leicester, Devonshire, and even the Emerald Isle; so that to spend an hour in a public-house . . . one might have heard a perfect babble of different dialects.' Outsiders, even immigrants from overseas – Jews, Germans and, especially after the Great Famine of the 1840s, Irish – flooded in to swell the population of the cities of the West Riding and subtly alter the character of urban Yorkshire.

Heathcliff's origin is unknown, and in the course of *Wuthering Heights*, he is showered with all sorts of

No one who came to Yorkshire around the turn of the century could fail to appreciate the bluff pride and down-to-earth manner of the wool craftsmen of the West Riding and their families. Emily Brontë must have seen such folk, for well into the 20s there were something like a thousand small master clothiers and weavers working away in the cramped cottages of Haworth, and their frequent comings and goings on business must have made the tiny, cluttered village into a bustling, active place.

DECLINE AND FALL

By then, however, the fortunes of the woolcraftsman were sinking fast beneath the rising tide of the Industrial Revolution, as factory after factory went up in the big cities of the West Riding to manufacture wool on a massive scale. The affluent independence of the wool-craftsmen was reduced to abject poverty almost overnight, for they stood no chance against the great factories. The factories employed hundreds of workers at starvation wages to operate steam-powered machines and monopolized both the supply of raw wool and the sale of finished cloth.

The wool croppers – once the aristocrats of the wool trade – had already gone under. They had fought desperately against the introduction of the cropping frames in factories which threw thousands of them out of work, but to no avail – one of the worst of the 'Luddite' riots against the new machines was in Patrick Brontë's own parish of Hartshead in 1812, and Emily's father must have been aware of the ruthless way the rioters were dealt with. In the 1820s and 30s, when Emily was living in Haworth, it was the weavers who were plunged into beggary by the extension of the factory system, and the introduction of the 'labour-saving' Jacquard power-loom.

Yorkshire collieries
Steel furnaces and the railways sent the demand for Yorkshire coal rocketing. But there was no shortage of hands ready to work in the pits – men, women and children. The picture above, entitled 'Pitmen at Play' almost achieves the impossible in sentimentalizing the harsh life these miners led – Yorkshire pits were notoriously unsafe.

epithets: he is a vagrant, a gypsy, "a little Lascar, or an Armenian or Spanish castaway". But his character may well have been suggested by the Irish children who arrived with their starving families at Liverpool, where Mr Earnshaw finds the little child – and where, in reality, Branwell Brontë must have seen them dying in the streets when he visited the city in 1845.

Few of the immigrants were as lucky as Heathcliff; most faced conditions as bad, if not worse, than those they had fled. With so many willing hands, the factories were able to pay workers less than a pittance, and lay them off at will. A bitter strike of 20,000 woolcombers and weavers in Bradford in 1825 for better conditions ended in disaster – partly because when the strike became a struggle for union recognition, the employers sacked all the children whose parents supported the idea of a trade union.

Men, women and children were forced to work long hours in exhausting, dangerous jobs for abysmal wages in the factories, and in the new coal mines which

Up at the big house
Life was good among the merchant classes. Great status was to be won by sheer financial success. A man had absolute power within his own home, and might achieve advantageous 'mergers' by means of his children's marriages. In many respects, his life resembled the privilege of the landed gentry, though the aristocracy liked to look down on those in 'trade' as jumped-up nouveaux riches.

Urban sprawl
Canals and railways brought raw materials to the factory door. And the workforce, too, had to move close to their only hope of employment. Families drifted in from the countryside – many made homeless by the notorious 'Enclosures Act' – to rows of bleak, back-to-back houses. The blight of such housing still scars many Yorkshire towns today.

were covering the landscape of the West Riding with slag heaps and soot. Crawling on all fours, far underground in a choking atmosphere, girls and boys of all ages from 7 to 21 would work in the mines virtually naked, dragging coal along with 'belts round their waists and a chain passing between their legs'.

The conditions these folk lived in were equally terrible. Most ex-weavers and their families dressed in rags, slept fitfully in sheds completely bare of any furniture but a stool or two, and, according to the Bradford social reformer Richard Oastler, 'they do not know what it is to taste flesh meat'. Worse still, the cities were unbelievably filthy and unhealthy, and working men died, on average, at only 19-20 years old while almost half the children died before the age of six. Back in the villages, conditions were little better, though the air was clean, and a report in 1840 showed that Haworth was one of the filthiest, most disease-ridden towns in England.

UNREST AND PROTEST
Naturally, the working class people protested every now and then about their conditions, and it is hardly surprising that the Chartist movement had widespread support in Yorkshire – though their activities were dealt with brutally and 'efficiently' by the army. 'Trouble at t'mill' became an all too familiar phrase for the Yorkshire mill-owner. There were philanthropic mill-owners, such as the grand textile baron, Sir Titus Salt, who set up a 'model' mill, away from the smoke of Bradford, at Saltaire. But such enlightened men were all too rare.

Some mill-owners, like Salt, were self-made men in the traditional Yorkshire mould – master clothiers and craftsmen who had built up their businesses from humble beginnings. Living in large, lavishly decorated

The grand hunts
In southern England, and in the refinement of the cities, the Yorkshire squires were written off as coarse country bumpkins. Within the Ridings, however, a man's worth was often judged by his horsemanship and the calibre of his dogs. The Yorkshire calendar was marked in terms of traditional hunting days and the annual hunt balls.

houses, and adopting the aristocracy's taste for art and for hunting, they still retained their blunt manner and, often, their Yorkshire dialect. Despite their wealth, and their often genuine refinement, they were frequently shunned by the traditional land-owning aristocracy – unless, of course, hard times encouraged a prudent match. Brought up in genteel poverty, the Brontë sisters too tended to scorn the virtues of the wealthy self-made man, regarding him as rather coarse.

For a generation or two, the mill-owners were not regarded as wholly acceptable to polite society. Then the influence of public (private) school was brought to bear on their sons, producing an upper class in which squires and manufacturers shared identical manners, morals and tastes and were hard to tell apart.

LIVES OF QUALITY

The self-made manufacturers, however, were always in the minority, for it was the landowners who had the capital and influence to set up an industrial enterprise. They built their houses in town at first, it is true, often on the hill overlooking their factory. But when the towns became too dirty, they readily moved out to country estates and joined in – and even monopolized – the old rural pursuits.

Of all the rural pursuits, none was more popular than hunting, and the Yorkshire squires were renowned for their enthusiasm for chasing foxes – though few could match the ardour of Lord Darlington, leader of the famous Raby Hunt, who was in the saddle nearly every day of his life for over 50 years. The ladies, meanwhile, and the less energetic gentlemen, would resort to the quiet elegance of spa towns such as Harrogate and Skipton to take the waters

for their health and join the sophisticated social round.

Without a doubt, the land itself influenced the Brontës as much as the people it bred. The bleak, uncomprising wildness of the moors, consorting with the almost domestic gentleness of the Dale Valley farms maintain a presence in Emily's novel as powerful as any male-female entanglement. The extreme climate, particularly winter, held a far greater significance than modern town-dwellers can easily appreciate. The cold, wind and wet were life-threatening adversaries. Indeed, they only could be said to have triumphed over those daughters of Yorkshire, the Brontë sisters.

The Peterloo Massacre
(below) In August, 1819, 11 people died and over 400 were injured by troops at a protest meeting at St Peter's Fields, Manchester. (The carnage was compared to that on the battlefield of Waterloo.) Such protests were met with similar brutality in Yorkshire.

ELIZABETH GASKELL

→ *1810-1865* →

From a witty, talkative, vivacious beauty, Elizabeth Gaskell matured into
a woman of astounding energy and hard-won experience. The poverty and
injustice she witnessed set her writing, but she never let literature outweigh
the other aspects of her busy life. Given her sociable nature and social
conscience, her time was already full. But, beset by demands for her work,
she laboured on, despite her over-taxed health, to preserve in the words and
images of fiction a disappearing world she valued for its charm and
innocence.

Faith, Hope and Charity

Principled, humorous and strong in her Unitarian belief, Mrs Gaskell took action in words and deeds to redress social wrongs and overcome seemingly insurmountable barriers.

Elizabeth Gaskell's character and talent were the product of a fostered childhood, of a stimulating and free-thinking religion, of rural peace and urban suffering, of domestic routine and poignant personal loss. The woman who emerged was energetic and positive, an observant, cultured artist, a classless friend to the famous and unknown alike, and above all a devoted wife and mother.

In her early 30s she wrote, on receiving some of her dead mother's letters from a family friend: 'I think no-one but one so unfortunate as to be early motherless can enter into the craving one has after the lost mother.' Yet despite her own early loss, Elizabeth's childhood was a very contented one. She was born Elizabeth Cleghorn Stevenson on 29 September 1810 in Chelsea. Her mother, worn out by giving birth to eight children – of whom only Elizabeth and her brother John survived – died 13 months later. Elizabeth's father, William, a Unitarian and the Keeper of the Treasury Records, was overwhelmed by the prospect of caring for such a

small child on his own, and gratefully seized on his sister-in-law's suggestion that Elizabeth should go and live with her in Knutsford, Cheshire.

Until she was 14, Elizabeth lived a happy and sheltered life in her aunt Hannah Lumb's large red-brick house, on the edge of the common in Knutsford. The house was really a little farm, with pigs, poultry, geese and a vegetable garden, and here Elizabeth learned the arts of housekeeping and cooking.

When her domestic duties were done, she spent hours reading or sewing in some nook or cranny of the house, or in the shade of an old fir tree on the front lawn. Often she joined the host of cousins who lived in nearby Sandlebridge, for a picnic or an outing. She also went with her uncle on his doctor's rounds of the local villages, and taught at Sunday school, as well as attending the Unitarian chapel. It was a peaceful, predictable atmosphere of provincial life.

Her visits to her father in London were in sharp contrast to this country idyll. William Stevenson remarried

Key Dates

1810 born in Chelsea

1811 moves to Aunt Lumb's in Cheshire

1832 marries William Gaskell

1840 first writing published by William Howitt

1848 *Mary Barton*

1850 commissioned by Dickens; meets Charlotte Brontë

1853 *Cranford*

1857 meets Charles Eliot Norton

1865 dies at Alton, Hampshire

A London birthplace
(far left) Elizabeth was born at fashionable Cheyne Walk, Chelsea (then Lindsey Row), overlooking the Thames.

Benevolent influences
Hannah Lumb (right) and Dr Peter Holland (far right), her mother's sister and brother, were devoted surrogate parents to 'Lily', as they called her. She was often to be seen accompanying her uncle, the local surgeon, on his neighbourhood rounds.

A country girl
(left) On her mother's death, Elizabeth (aged one year) was sent to live with her aunt at Knutsford, Cheshire. She thrived on the wholesome, tranquil atmosphere, and here established her life-long love of literature and of the countryside.

'Cranford'
This picture (below), taken in 1865, shows the High Street of Mrs Gaskell's home town of Knutsford, which was the inspiration for her most famous novel.

Courtesy of Mrs. Trevor Jones

This news devastated Elizabeth's father and he requested her company immediately. For the next two years, Elizabeth was part of the Stevenson household and nursed her father through failing health and a stroke, until he died in 1829. After this she seems to have broken almost entirely with her stepfamily, not seeing them again for 25 years.

A COMPASSIONATE NATURE

Elizabeth spent the next two winters in Newcastle, at the home of a distant family connection, a Unitarian minister and teacher, William Turner. He was greatly revered in the town for his commitment to cultural and philanthropic improvements. The Unitarian faith in principle stood for freedom of thought and action, and these ideals infused Elizabeth's philosophy all her life. William Turner's brand of active, charitable religion formed a blueprint for Elizabeth's own. She was compassionate by nature, and her religion was always motivated by an unaffected desire to help others. Neither dogmatic nor censorious, her zeal was never at odds with her irrepressible sense of fun and gaiety.

An outbreak of cholera in Newcastle sent Elizabeth and William Turner's daughter, Anne, to seek the safety of Edinburgh, where Elizabeth's beauty and vivacity attracted attention. On her return to Knutsford in 1831, 21-year-old Elizabeth visited William Turner's daughter Mary, who lived in Manchester. Mary's hus-

in 1814 and had two more children, William and Catherine. Of her visits to London Elizabeth said in later life, '. . . *very, very* unhappy I used to be; and if it had not been for the beautiful, grand river which was an inexplicable comfort to me . . . I think my child's heart would have broken'.

At the age of 13, Elizabeth went as a boarder to Avonbank school in Stratford-upon-Avon, which was run by her stepmother's relatives, the Misses Byerley. Here she stayed for three years without returning to Knutsford, and seems to have been perfectly happy learning languages, deportment and etiquette – the traditional subjects for a young lady of her day.

In 1827 Elizabeth returned to Knutsford – but not for long. In August 1828, she received a letter from her brother John, a mariner with the East India Company. He wrote that he was setting sail for a new life in India, and concluded, 'Should we never meet again, accept my very best wishes for your welfare through life and may every blessing attend you'. Shortly afterwards he was reported missing, presumed drowned at sea.

Mansell Collection

THE HIGH STREET "CRANFORD" 1865

band was the senior minister at the Unitarian Cross Street Chapel. His junior minister, William Gaskell, was a serious and learned man who was to make his name as a German scholar, a Professor of English History and Literature, an authority on Lancastrian dialect and a writer of hymns.

Elizabeth and William felt a swift mutual attraction, despite a seemingly radical difference in character which caused Aunt Lumb to say jokingly, 'How could the man ever take a fancy to such a little, giddy, thoughtless thing as you?' Elizabeth's 'wonderful' incessant conversation was later described by one of her husband's pupils as 'like the gleaming ripple and rush of a clear deep stream in sunshine'.

The couple were married in Knutsford Parish Church on 30 August 1832. Following the local custom, the villagers sprinkled red sand outside their houses and decorated this with flowers of white sand, in their honour. After a month's blissful honeymoon in Wales, the Gaskells settled in Manchester at 14 Dover Street.

Now Elizabeth had to draw on all her resources to cope – emotionally and practically – with the desperate privations she witnessed among her husband's mill-worker parishioners. As a minister's wife – and as the woman she was – she could not but be deeply involved in attempts to help them. But she was faced with poverty that could not be alleviated by simple charity. At this time, a mill-worker might have an income of 1/6d per week with which to feed, house and clothe his family. Most lived in one-room hovels and watched their babies die one by one.

Mrs Gaskell's own first child was still-born, but in September 1834 she bore a daughter, baptized Marianne but always known as Ma or Minnie. Meta,

the Gaskells' second daughter, was born in February 1837. In May of the same year, her beloved Aunt Lumb died, leaving a sudden void in Elizabeth's life – 'Oh there never will be one like her'. But Aunt Lumb left her a legacy of £80 a year – a great help to the Gaskells' finances.

FIRST WRITING

At about this time, Mrs Gaskell made a tentative start on her writing career. She wrote to William Howitt, a famous contemporary author, after reading about a book he and his wife were compiling: *Visits to Remarkable Places*. She asked him if one of her favourite school-day haunts, Old Clopton Hall, was to be included, and vividly described it. Indeed, it *was* included, and in her own words.

William Howitt insisted that she should devote herself to writing full-time – an impracticable suggestion for the hard-working wife of a minister. However, the correspondence between the two started a lasting friendship. This was consolidated when, in 1841, the Gaskells' circumstances improved sufficiently to allow them to visit the Rhine, where the Howitts had settled. Mrs Gaskell was so impressed by the Howitts' splendid residence in Heidelberg, that she wrote to a friend, 'My word! authorship brings them in a pretty penny'.

In 1842 another daughter, Florence Elizabeth (Flossy), was born and the Gaskells moved to 121 Upper Rumford Street to accommodate the growing family. A baby boy, William, was born in 1844 and Mrs Gaskell's days followed a tranquil ritual of domestic routine. William was especially dear to her, and she later wrote, '. . . so affectionate and *reasonable* a baby I never saw'.

The following year, however, while the family was

An attraction of opposites

Elizabeth (below right) is shown here at the age of 21, the time at which she met her future husband, William Gaskell, a Unitarian minister (below). Despite their contrasting personalities (he was shy and scholarly, she 'giddy and thoughtless'), they fell deeply in love and married after a courtship of months. An unusually liberal Victorian husband, William encouraged Elizabeth to write her first novel, Mary Barton, *and helped her to weather the storm of criticism that her candid, pioneering brand of writing aroused.*

National Portrait Gallery, London

John Rylands University Library of Manchester

LOST AT SEA

Mrs Gaskell's older brother, John Stevenson, disappeared on a sea voyage to India in 1828. This tragedy is often reflected in her writing, notably in the similar disappearance of Peter Jenkyns that casts a shadow over Miss Matty's life in *Cranford*, and adds to the poignancy of her solitary suffering.

A twist was added to Mrs Gaskell's own loss in that her brother was rumoured to have survived and landed at Calcutta. And in her fiction – for instance, *Sylvia's Lovers* – Mrs Gaskell devised a happy ending to the incident, perhaps willing that her own beloved brother might one day reappear in England, safe and sound. But despite this element of wish-fulfilment in her writing, her nautical characters have a freshness and authenticity that come from first-hand experience.

George H. Boughton: Memories. Royal Academy of Arts

on holiday in Wales, 10-month-old William died of scarlet fever. Mrs Gaskell was so overcome that her own life was thought to be in jeopardy, and her husband searched desperately for some means of rousing her from her grief and depression. He suggested she write a book, and so it was that her personal sorrow became interwoven with the extreme poverty she saw daily in Manchester. The novel that evolved was *Mary Barton*. Although flawed in some respects, it owes much of its power to a bereft woman's urgent need to ease her own anguish, and to her compassionate insight into the conditions of the working class.

The birth of her fourth daughter, Julia Bradford, in September 1846, was a further comfort but, when moving house four years later, Elizabeth was still referring to the memories evoked by their previous home – 'the precious perfume lingering of my darling's short presence in this life'.

Meanwhile, with her novel awaiting publication, Mrs Gaskell published three short stories in William Howitt's journal, under the pen-name Cotton Mather Mills, Esq. This attempt to protect her identity was partly to avoid causing trouble to her husband, who preached to the wealthy mill-owners she criticized, as

Marianne, Meta and Flossie

This drawing (below) shows Mrs Gaskell's three eldest daughters in 1845. In that year, Mrs Gaskell was devastated by the death of her baby William, her only son. She later said, 'one evil of this bustling life [is] that one never has time calmly and bravely to face a great grief'.

Sir Hubert von Herkomer: Hard Times. Manchester City Art Gallery/Bridgeman Art Library

The plight of the poor

In the 'Hungry Forties', Manchester was the heart of the industrial north; people flooded into the city from the surrounding countryside (left), in search of work. They found only squalor, unemployment and high levels of infant mortality. The Gaskells worked daily with the city's poor, teaching, feeding and clothing them. These experiences gave direction and insight to Mrs Gaskell's early novels, and a contemporary critic wrote: 'Do they [the rich] want to know why poor men . . . learn to hate law and order . . . to hate the rich, in short? Then let them read Mary Barton.'

Courtesy of Mrs. Trevor Jones

City of contrasts

'Rightly understood, Manchester is as great a human exploit as Athens', wrote Disraeli, and for many it seemed a city of opportunities. But another contemporary account pointed out, 'there is no town in the world where the distance between the rich and the poor is so great'. Mrs Gaskell knew both sides intimately.

well as the poor mill-workers she championed. Mrs Gaskell was pleasantly surprised, however, when one manufacturer actually thanked her for portraying him so faithfully!

The success of her first novel brought Mrs Gaskell to social prominence, and she found herself in London, dining with Dickens and meeting Thackeray, as well as corresponding with Carlyle. Dickens was keen for Mrs Gaskell to contribute to his new journal, *Household Words*. And so, *Cranford* was born.

Mrs Gaskell and Charlotte Brontë met for the first time shortly before *Cranford*'s success, at the house of a mutual acquaintance. Elizabeth described Charlotte – in mourning for Emily, Anne and Branwell – as 'the little lady in the black silk gown', while Charlotte thought

Mrs Gaskell was 'a woman of the most genuine talent — of cheerful, pleasing and cordial manners and — I believe — of a kind and good heart'.

Their lifestyles were in marked contrast. Mrs Gaskell ran a large, bustling household with children and several servants. Charlotte Brontë, the unmarried daughter of a most difficult father, lived a life of seclusion in the wild setting of Haworth. Yet even though Charlotte and Mrs Gaskell seem never to have been on first-name terms, they became good friends, visiting each other and maintaining a regular correspondence, at least until Charlotte's marriage in 1854. And when Charlotte died in 1855, it was Mrs Gaskell whom Mr Brontë asked to write his daughter's biography.

Mrs Gaskell's *Life of Charlotte Brontë* was published in

FLORENCE NIGHTINGALE

'The lady with the lamp', Florence Nightingale, forged the modern concept of nursing in the field hospitals of the Crimea. Mrs Gaskell met her in 1854 and found her 'like a saint'. 'She has no friend – she wants none. She stands perfectly alone, halfway between God and his creatures.' But Mrs Gaskell disagreed with her ideas on child-rearing (that it should not be done by the mother), and once related how they 'had a grand quarrel one day. She is, I think, too much for institutions . . .'

The Nightingale family were kind to Mrs Gaskell, inviting her to their Derbyshire home to write *North and South* in the seclusion of a 'turret . . . a quarter of a mile of stair cases . . . away from everyone in the house'. She enjoyed this quiet time, calling it 'my happy, happy pause of life'.

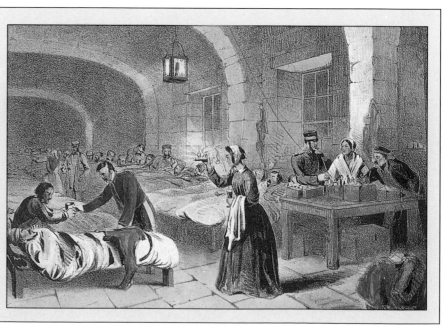

I. Caffi: Morning, Monte Pincio, Ca' Pesaro, Venice/Scala

The Brontë Society

Roman spring
One of Mrs Gaskell's most memorable holidays was her visit to Rome (left) with her daughters, when she met Charles Eliot Norton, an American intellectual. He was 16 years her junior, but the rapport between them was immediate and lasting.

A fellow writer
Mrs Gaskell met Charlotte Brontë (right) in 1850, and they formed a friendship based on mutual liking and respect. The biography which Mrs Gaskell wrote after Charlotte's death stirred up a 'hornets' nest' of controversy – but has borne out Mr Brontë's opinion that it would be 'in the first rank of Biographies till the end of time . . .'

1857 and is considered by some to be one of the finest biographies in English literature. George Eliot found it 'as poetic as one of her [Mrs Gaskell's] own novels', and there does seem to have been a certain amount of creative licence involved in its writing. The first edition had to be withdrawn so that various offending passages relating to Mr Brontë, Rev. Nicholls (Charlotte's husband), the servants and a widow who may have had an affair with Branwell Brontë, could be removed.

Initially, Mrs Gaskell was blissfully unaware of the uproar caused by her book, as she was holidaying in Rome with two of her daughters. Here she met Charles Eliot Norton, a young Unitarian intellectual from America, on a European tour. He was a great admirer of Mrs Gaskell's work, and they spent several happy weeks of a magical spring in Rome. In this short time, a deep and intense friendship grew up between them, and they exchanged little notes daily in addition to their meetings. All too soon the idyllic interlude was over. Mrs Gaskell returned to England to face a barrage of correspondence about *The Life of Charlotte Brontë*. Norton returned to America, where he eventually married, but the two maintained a regular correspondence until Mrs Gaskell's death.

LATER LIFE

As her children grew up, Mrs Gaskell was able to allow herself the luxury of time devoted solely to writing. She was invited by Florence Nightingale's family, for example, to seclude herself at their house, Lea Hurst in Derbyshire, to work on *North and South*.

Travel was to be a feature of Elizabeth's later life, and a long sojourn in Whitby furnished the material for *Sylvia's Lovers*. Most of her travels were undertaken without her husband, who refused to be parted from his work, except for the occasional solitary holiday abroad. Mrs Gaskell herself went abroad frequently, often with her daughters, visiting France and Germany. Much of

BBC Hulton Picture Library

Wives and Daughters was written while visiting the eccentric Parisian hostess, Mme Mohl.

But she still spent much time on her arduous duties as a minister's wife. In 1862, after tireless work among the famine-struck mill-workers, she and her daughters spent a short period of recuperation at Eastbourne. She suffered increasingly from fatigue and strain, but she cheered herself up by purchasing a large house and four acres of land at Alton in Hampshire. This was initially to be a secret from William Gaskell, for she hoped to be able to persuade him to retire there. Sadly, she was never to live in her country home. Nor was she ever to finish her final novel, *Wives and Daughters*. The last lines she wrote for its serialization in *Cornhill Magazine* were, 'and now cover me up close and let me go to sleep, and dream about my dear Cynthia and my new shawl'.

On 12 November 1865, while visiting her new house with her son-in-law and two daughters, Mrs Gaskell died suddenly but peacefully, while taking tea in the afternoon.

A final home
'The house is large, . . . in a very pretty garden . . . and in the middle of a pretty rural village', wrote Mrs Gaskell of 'The Lawn', at Alton in Hampshire (below). She bought the house – from the proceeds of her writing – as a surprise for her husband, and hoped to retire there. But her plan was never to be realized. She died suddenly, on her first visit to the house, during Sunday tea by the drawing-room fire.

CRANFORD

Left behind by a fast-moving world, the ladies of Cranford have little but etiquette and pride to arm them against the small crises and deeper tragedies of their bitter-sweet lives.

ranford is a wonderfully detailed account of life in a small country town during the early 19th century. There is subtlety of tone in almost every line of the book: a tender, delicate mocking of lifestyles and values that invites us to marvel and sympathize with the eccentric ways of all the Cranford characters and the 'elegant economy' they are obliged to practise. The novel is a riveting study of a changing, disappearing world which the author was anxious to capture. Mrs Gaskell was not writing about her contemporaries, but about people she had known in her childhood.

The book is intensely moving in parts, but also extremely funny. Mrs Gaskell herself confessed, 'It is the only one of my own books

> " 'Elegant economy!' How naturally one falls back into the phraseology of Cranford! There, economy was always 'elegant,' and money-spending always 'vulgar and ostentatious;' a sort of sour grapeism, which made us very peaceful and satisfied."

that I can read again . . . whenever I am ailing or ill, I take *Cranford* and . . . laugh over it afresh!'

GUIDE TO THE PLOT

Genteel society in Cranford is made up of unmarried or widowed middle-aged women, ironically named the 'Amazons' in the opening chapter. The book centres on the home of sisters Deborah and Matilda Jenkyns, daughters of the long-dead rector. They live quietly on their modest income, entertaining friends with tea, bread and butter and card games in the evening.

Their routine is upset by the arrival of the loud, bluff Captain Brown and his two daughters. His kindness and sound advice soon outweigh his appalling lack of tact in admitting to poverty. Unfortunately, his delight in Dickens arouses Miss Deborah's old-fashioned literary prejudices. She pronounces Dr Johnson the better writer and is unable to forgive the captain for disagreeing with her. Miss Jenkyns even attributes the tragedy which befalls him to his infatuation with Dickens.

Incidents of Cranford life are seen through the eyes of young Mary Smith, a visitor from Drumble, the nearby industrial city. Her sharp and lively observations set the tone of the novel. For example, she notices that after the death of the austere elder sister Deborah, poor Miss Matty finds simple everyday decisions difficult to face. But gradually we discover, along with Mary, the tragedy that lies at the root of her helplessness – of her thwarted love affair with a neighbouring farmer. Miss Matty's reaction to the unexpected reappearance of her former suitor leads Mary Smith to reflect "how faithful her poor

Society "in possession of the Amazons"
A community of spinsters and widows, the ladies of Cranford derive their excitement from house-calls, card-games (left), Sunday service and above all, harmless gossipy scandal.

heart had been in its sorrow and its silence".

Sorting through old letters prompts Miss Matty to tell the story of her younger brother, Peter who left home under a cloud. A wild, appealing boy, his childhood ended abruptly with one prank too many – a prank which drove him out of Cranford. He is believed dead – drowned at sea – although Miss Matty confesses, "when I sit by myself, and all the house is still, I think I hear his step coming up the street, and my heart begins to flutter and beat . . ."

The arrival of a real member of the aristoc-

Caps and turbans
The greatest concession the impoverished heroines can make to the dictates of fashion is a new cap (above) or the reworking of an old one – though at one time Miss Matty looks likely to disfigure "her small gentle mousey face with a great Saracen head turban".

racy, sister-in-law to the lazy, overweight Mrs Jamieson, brings great excitement, especially when Lady Glenmire turns out to be far more approachable and down-to-earth than seems quite proper for a Baron's widow. In fact, for a time, her behaviour condemns her to exclusion from Cranford gatherings – a matter only rectified in the final chapter.

More excitement occurs with a visit from Signor Brunoni, a real live conjuror, whose wonderful tricks amaze everyone but the sceptical Miss Pole. And Signor Brunoni's wife has tales to tell of a bygone life in India,

Giving way to love
Beset by their "dread of men and matrimony", the householders forbid their women servants to have 'followers'. But Matty, stirred by her renewed acquaintance with the man she once hoped to marry, lifts the ban on her resourceful young servant, Martha (above).

Captain Brown
The likeable, retired military man and his two very different daughters (left) were at the heart of Mrs Gaskell's first episode of Cranford. *Initially, no book was envisaged, and she later admitted, 'I never meant to write more, so killed Captain Brown very much against my will'.*

Unstoppable progress
Captain Brown works for the new railway (right) – a hated intrusion. It is, ironically, this symbol of modern progress that robs Cranford of its gentle hero.

including some details which set Mary Smith off on a detective's trail.

Disaster looms for Miss Matty when the Town and Country Bank collapses, reducing her savings to a pittance. Her friends rally round, however, and she is persuaded to earn a genteel living. The book ends on a happy note, with a reunion which brings "Peace to Cranford" at last.

PERIOD CHARM

Cranford began as a series of self-contained sketches, which Mrs Gaskell later worked together to make the novel – and which account for its episodic structure. Contemporary critics described her book as 'delicate', 'tender', 'exquisite', a piece of 'social painting' full of charm. Certainly the book celebrates old-world innocence, and on one level can be enjoyed simply as a delightful period piece. The pages abound with humorous descriptions of daily rituals, which are made all the more amusing by the simple fact that the characters remain quite unaware of how they must appear:

"The card-table was an animated scene to watch; four ladies' heads, with niddle-nodding caps, all nearly meeting over the middle of the table, in their eagerness to whisper quick enough and loud enough . . ."

But while Mrs Gaskell invites us to smile at the odd habits of her characters she is always careful to show the human or social reality behind their eccentricities. They are not just figures of fun. Cranford ladies wear "well preserved, old fashioned clothes", arguing " 'What does it signify how we dress here at Cranford, where everybody knows us?' And if they go from home, their reason is equally cogent: 'What does it signify how we dress here, where nobody knows us?' "

The harsh truth is that no-one has enough money to live in the style to which they aspire, and so all kinds of peculiar fictions are maintained to disguise the 'shameful' face of poverty. Old worn caps and collars are kept for indoor wear, hastily changed when visitors knock. Candles are only lit seconds before visitors arrive, and everyone always pretends to be surprised at the cakes produced with tea, even the mistress of the house, "though she knew, and we knew, and she knew that we knew, and we knew that she knew we knew, she had been busy all the morning making tea-bread and sponge cakes."

HIDDEN TRAGEDY

Other serious truths lie half-hidden beneath the rules of etiquette that govern the genteel Cranford circle. Slowly we learn of the deep

tragedy of Miss Matty's life. Her helplessness in the opening chapters is at once understandable and forgivable as it becomes clear that the domination of her father and sister has ruined her life. As a young woman she loses her mother, her brother – and later her lover

> *" . . . we used to make a regular expedition all round the kitchens and cellars every night, Miss Matty leading the way, armed with the poker, I following with the hearth-brush, and Martha carrying the shovel and fire-irons with which to sound the alarm . . ."*

Holbrook, whom her father and sister force her to reject because of his humble origins. She apologetically confides late one evening to Mary Smith:

"I dream sometimes that I have a little child – always the same – a little girl of about two years old . . . she comes to me when she is very sorry or very glad, and I have wakened with the clasp of her dear little arms round my neck."

This is as near as Mrs Gaskell comes to sen-

In the Background

BANK FAILURE

During the late 18th century, bankers made loans of banknotes rather than actual gold. In fact they issued notes with a nominal value 10 times more than the gold they held, When Government gold reserves were swallowed up by the Napoleonic Wars, the Bank of England became unable to cash notes on demand. From 1797 to 1819 all cash payments were suspended. When the suspension was lifted, holders rushed to cash their notes, and many small, private county banks went bankrupt.

Personal ruin
Cranford illustrates Mrs Gaskell's skill at showing the impact on individual lives of such faults in the economic system. Miss Matty's income falls to £13 a year when her bank fails (below).

timentality and it is always tempered by the plausibility of the character speaking and the harsh truth that people did in fact lead such impoverished lives.

Times are changing. Mary Smith, fresh from the hustling, energetic city, feels Miss Matty's sadness keenly, and expresses impatience with the values that have undoubtedly caused her cruel suffering. There is a feeling that such a thing would not happen now. Cranford ladies have always been suspicious of the state of matrimony: "A man, is *so* in the way in the house!" But Miss Matty, in re-living the sorrow of her lost love, relents and allows her servant Martha to have a 'follower': "God forbid! . . . that I should grieve any young hearts." Lady Glenmire breaks a taboo by marrying Mr Hoggins, taking his name and forsaking her title. When she hears of the wedding, Miss Matty's response is fearful but excited, "Two people that we know going to be married. It's coming very near!"

DISQUIETING CHANGE

However much Cranford and its inhabitants may choose to ignore the vast economic and social changes taking place in England at that time, they cannot remain unaffected. Behind the Cranford façade of aristocratic dignity, hovers a collection of ageing women, increasingly unable to continue in the way they have always done. New influences are creeping in. These began with the arrival of Captain Brown in the opening chapters of the book. Miss Jenkyns and her Johnsonian sentences must make way for Dickens. The railway has come close to Cranford despite having been "vehemently petitioned against by the little town". Rumours of dangerous gangs roaming the countryside threaten the "genteel and well-bred" citizens, who are used to lying snugly in bed, secure in the belief that theirs is "an honest and moral town". Even the bank that held the Misses Jenkyns' investments for so long, crashes, taking everything with it.

It is this opposition between two contrasting worlds which Mrs Gaskell so carefully and painstakingly explores in *Cranford*. The narrow, stultifying world of the town itself, with its snobbishness and petty moral sensibility must – sooner or later – make way for the more vital, energetic forces of the new age. Nevertheless, many of its old-fashioned human qualities are worth preserving. Miss Matty, Miss Pole and their friends, are motivated by true kindness and generosity – the very virtues that the new industrial world lacks. As Mary Smith wryly observes:

". . . *my father says 'such simplicity might be very well in Cranford, but would never do in the*

"Don't leave me!"
Despite stories of robber bands, the friends brave Darkness Lane at night. Matty, voted into the only sedan chair (above), begs the bearers "not to run away and leave her . . . to be murdered".

world.' And I fancy the world must be very bad, for with all my father's suspicion of every one with whom he has dealings, and in spite of all his many precautions, he lost upwards of a thousand pounds by roguery only last year."

We are left hoping that there is some place in the future where the best that it is to be found in Cranford can survive. "We all love Miss Matty, and I somehow think we are all of us better when she is near us."

"The Aga Jenkyns"
The much-travelled Brunonis recollect a "kind Englishman . . . [amid] the natives" of Chunderabaddad, India (left). Could it be that Matty's missing sailor brother did not really drown at sea nor become Lama of Tibet?

Shopping trips
The little shop in Cranford (above) is a rendezvous, and a source of entertainment and news – though little ready money crosses the counter. Small wonder that Matty is excited when she goes to buy her one dress of the year.

Cat and collar
Mrs Forrester confides how washing her best lace collar in milk led to it being eaten by the cat. Such a disaster called for bold measures – but, after a dose of currant-jelly and tartar emetic, the lace was restored to its owner (right).

CHARACTERS IN FOCUS

All the major characters in *Cranford* are upper middle-class and eager to claim aristocratic connection wherever possible. Their place in the social hierarchy dictates the pattern of their daily lives. But in Mrs Gaskell's skilful hands, their absurd pride and prejudices invite only fond mockery.

Through the emerging story of Miss Matty's life, hidden depths of passion and grief add a greater dimension to our appreciation and understanding of all these quaint characters and their comical, outmoded world.

WHO'S WHO

Miss Matty — The gentle, endearing 'heroine' of the novel.

Mary Smith — The almost anonymous narrator, a generation or more younger than her friend Miss Matty – a link between the old world and the new industrial one.

Signor Brunoni — An exotic touring conjuror, who is not all he appears . . .

Mrs Jamieson — The most lazy, wealthy, aristocratic, ignorant and prejudiced of the Cranford set.

Lady Glenmire — Unpretentious widow of a Scottish baron, she is only too willing to mix and make friends with everyone.

Martha — "A rought, honest-looking country-girl". When she enters Matty's service, she becomes her fiercely loyal friend.

Miss Jenkyns — Matty's older sister, who "would have despised the modern idea of women being equal to men. Equal, indeed! she knew they were superior."

Peter Jenkyns — Matty's brother, once "too fond of mischief". He is still sorely missed long years after his disappearance.

Captain Brown — A half-pay captain, "so brazen as to talk of being poor", who wins respect and affection and soon has "his opinions quoted as authority" in Cranford.

Thomas Holbrook — A bluff but well-read farmer who, in his younger days, made an offer of marriage to Matty.

Mary Smith (right), with her detached, wry observations as narrator, and her evident affection for her Cranford friends, gives the book its distinctive tone of voice. Practical and down-to-earth, she is able to sort out many of her neighbours' problems and, on many occasions, unobtrusively has the last word: "I was right," she says, laughing also at herself, "I think that must be an hereditary quality, for my father says he is hardly ever wrong."

W.K. Blacklock: *A Quiet Read*, Anthony Mitchell Fine Paintings/Fine Art Photographic Library

Lady Glenmire (left), with her "very bright black eyes and a pleasant, sharp face; not over young" disarms the Cranford ladies. They have awaited her arrival with awed anticipation at the thought of mixing with nobility. She proves to be a refreshing contrast to Mrs Jamieson, her snobbish relation. As a newcomer, she is able to accept and reward goodwill wherever she finds it. But how will she react to the surgeon, rough Mr Hoggins?

Mansell Collection

G.B. O'Neill: The Jewel Casket/Fine Art Photographic Library

Walter Dendy Sadler: His Favourite Bin/Fine Art Photographic Library

Miss Matilda Jenkyns (left), affectionately known to all as Miss Matty, is living proof of "how a good innocent life makes friends all round". Her serving girl, Martha, adores her: "I'm not going to leave Miss Matty. No! not if she gives me warning every hour in the day!" But Matty's life is also a sad tale of lost opportunities. She admits, "I dream sometimes that I have a little child . . . she comes to me when she is very sorry or very glad, and I have wakened with the clasp of her dear little arms round my neck."

Mr Holbrook, yeoman farmer (above), is a picture of bluff good nature. "He despised every refinement which had not its roots deep down in humanity," but is far from uncultured. He is fond of "repeating apt and beautiful quotations from the poets" and displays an "ever increasing delight in the daily and yearly change of season and beauty." Miss Matty's nervous excitement at renewing his acquaintance and her tender anxieties over his planned trip to Paris ("I don't believe frogs will agree with him") hint at a long-repressed but unquenchable love for him.

"A magnificent gentleman in the Turkish costume" goes by the name of Signor Brunoni (left). He is revealed when the curtain rises on a much vaunted performance of magic in the Assembly Hall. "Seated before a little table, gazing at us . . . with calm and condescending dignity," he is a majestic figure. Later, "pale and feeble" after an accident and using his alias 'Samuel Brown', he arouses quite different emotions – ". . . it was wonderful to see what kind feelings were called out by this poor man's coming amongst us."

Frederick Goodall: The Pasha. Roy Miles Fine Paintings/Bridgeman Art Library

The Honourable Mrs Jamieson (right) "sits fat and inert, and very much at the mercy of her old servants . . .", but is the absolute arbiter in Cranford of what is "the thing" and what is "not the thing". Mary shrewdly observes, "What 'the thing' was, I never could find out, but it must have been something eminently dull and tiresome." All but Mary look on her as the local oracle, though she shows herself to be quite unworthy of such status ("quiet people have more quiet impertinence than others"). At the house-parties, when everyone else is animatedly playing cards and chattering, Mrs Jamieson can be relied upon to be found fast asleep or eating "with a placid, ruminating expression of countenance, not unlike a cow's."

FAMILY BEFORE FAME

Mrs Gaskell's writing attracted an avid readership, but she could not always keep up with the demand for her work. For she always put her husband and children first.

'I do not think I ever cared for literary fame; nor do I think it *is* a thing that ought to be cared for. It comes and it goes. The exercise of a talent or power *is* always a great pleasure; but one should weigh well whether this pleasure may not be obtained by the sacrifice of some duty. When I had *little* children I do not think I could have written stories, because I should have become too much absorbed in my *fictitious* people to attend to my *real* ones . . . everyone who tries to write stories *must* become absorbed in them (fictitious though they be) if they are to interest their readers . . .'

This extract from a letter of advice to a young hopeful, written towards the end of Mrs Gaskell's life, partly explains her late start in literature: 'When you are forty, and if you have a gift for being an authoress, you will write ten times as good a novel as you could do now, just because you will have gone through so much more of the interests of a wife and a mother.' Unlike Jane Austen, the Brontë sisters and George Eliot, Elizabeth Gaskell both benefited and suffered from domestic claims on her time and energy.

In reality, Mrs Gaskell did not follow her own advice to the letter, since she began her first novel *Mary Barton* in 1845, just before the birth of her youngest child. She did so with the encouragement of her husband, who believed that it would assuage her grief over the death of their little son. Her literary ability had already become apparent in her collaboration with her husband in composing poetry and researching lectures; in her ability to spin a fireside tale; and in her lively letters, dashed off between chores.

AN INDEPENDENT MIND

The Rev. William Gaskell's attitude was of decisive importance in Elizabeth's career. A reserved and somewhat aloof personality, he made no attempt to dominate his wife. In one of her letters she even complained laughingly that life was easier 'back in the darkness where obedience was the only seen duty of woman. Only even then I don't believe William would ever have *commanded* me.' The Unitarian tradition also helped. Whereas Charlotte Brontë's independent intellectual life ended with her marriage to the Anglican curate Arthur Nicholls, Mrs Gaskell belonged to a sect that favoured giving girls a sound education and was not hostile to feminine achievement.

The launching of Mrs Gaskell also owed

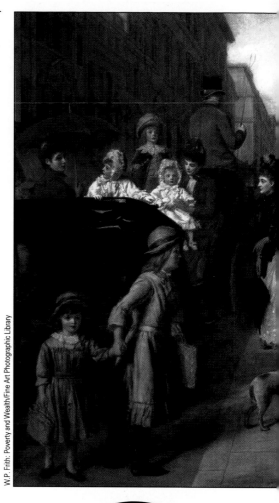

W.P. Frith: Poverty and Wealth/Fine Art Photographic Library

Courtesy of Mrs. Trevor Jones

Wife and mother
Mrs Gaskell's duties included educating her daughters: 'we shall work together, and read some book aloud . . . I shall give them dictation and grammar lessons, walk out with them . . . their companion and friend' (left). And although she was the professional writer of the family, only her husband (above) had a study; Mrs Gaskell had to make do with any convenient quiet spot.

W. S. Coleman: Happy Days/Fine Art Photographic Library

Class divisions
Mrs Gaskell was alarmed by the strength of feeling aroused by her political novels, which centred on social inequality: 'No one can feel more deeply than I how wicked it is to . . . excite class against class.'

Home truths
When she turned instead to earlier times and gentler subject matters, she drew on her intimate knowledge of provincial Knutsford. This shop (right) is the very one on which she styled Miss Matty's tea-and-sweets emporium in Cranford.

An eye for detail
A gifted artist, Mrs Gaskell drew this sketch (below) of Howarth parsonage to illustrate her Life of Charlotte Brontë.

Mansell Collection

much to a philanthropic journalist, William Howitt, with whom the Gaskells had become friendly. Howitt sent *Mary Barton* to John Forster, a reader for Chapman and Hall, who eventually published the book. He also negotiated the contract and, while Chapman and Hall delayed bringing out the novel, printed three stories by Mrs Gaskell in his short-lived *Howitt's Journal*.

Mrs Gaskell's extensive charitable work among the poor gave her first novels both their impetus and insight. *Mary Barton* displayed a sympathetic understanding of class resentment and of the urgent need for working people's wrongs to be redressed. Set back in time to the years of the Chartist movement, *Mary Barton* was not intended as a specifically political plea by Mrs Gaskell, but inevitably it had political implications. Manchester mill-owners and the Tory press were outraged, but Thomas Carlyle for one was both warm and perceptive in his praise of the author.

Ruth was conceived with a similarly humanitarian intention – that of awakening the public's conscience about prostitution. Inspired by a real-life story, Mrs Gaskell's frank treatment of an 'unmentionable' subject once more exposed her to further abuse – 'I am in a quiver of pain about it'. But she stood by the novel, and her husband and certain

friends gave her much-needed moral support.

One person who had been particularly impressed by *Mary Barton* was Charles Dickens, and he immediately asked its author to contribute to his periodical *Household Words*. Mrs Gaskell's story *Lizzie Leigh* was serialized in March/April 1850 and other stories followed. Dickens paid generously for these – and sent repeated requests for more material.

Mrs Gaskell now began drawing on her Knutsford memories to write the sketches which appeared in December 1851. 'The beginning of *Cranford* was *one* paper in *Household Words*, – and I never meant to write more'. But she did, at Dickens' insistence – and so her most famous novel was born.

Despite the outlet he gave her writing, Mrs Gaskell never really cared for Dickens,

although she greatly admired his work. He was too flamboyant and demanding for her taste; and the friction between contributor and editor became serious when *North and South* began to appear in *Household Words*.

Finding it hard to meet deadlines and impossible to devise a 'cliffhanger' ending for each episode, Mrs Gaskell complained that she was being forced to compress her story so rigorously that it was becoming nonsensical. For once, she even declared that she was 'sick of writing'. But the situation was at least as aggravating for Dickens, who was concerned to bring out his magazine regularly, and he exclaimed in exasperation, 'Mrs Gaskell, fearful – fearful. If I were Mr G., O Heaven how I would beat her!' Later, Mrs Gaskell found an alternative outlet in the *Cornhill Magazine,* founded by her publisher, George Smith. But she never quite broke free of Dickens.

North and South is sometimes seen as a retreat from the abrasive social criticism of *Mary Barton*. Mrs Gaskell was very much alarmed to think her work might cause vio-lent political protest (which she never intended). In the later book, the chief characters are middle – rather than working – class, and the message of kindness and reconciliation between classes is made abundantly clear. This may also owe something to an increased prosperity in Manchester in the 1850s which suggested grounds for optimism. Having written two 'industrial' books and the scandalous *Ruth*, Mrs Gaskell turned to less contentious moral and psychological subjects –

Holiday inspiration
A ten-day visit to the Yorkshire coast gave shape to Sylvia's Lovers. *Fictional Monkshaven is Whitby (below).*

Illustrious editor
'Dickens [right] writes to her praisingly'. But writer and editor often clashed, for she had difficulty meeting his magazine deadlines.

when she had time, health and energy to write.

Although William Gaskell was an exceptional Victorian husband, he made all the usual assumptions about the role of the man in the house – and Elizabeth never challenged them. William worked in a comfortable study, while his wife wrote wherever she could find temporary quiet. '*Women* must give up living an artist's life', she wrote, 'if home duties are to be paramount. It is different with men, whose home duties are so small a part of their life.' She had servants to do the menial work, but running the house, educating the girls, entertaining, and charitable activity made it impossible for Mrs Gaskell to produce literary work in an uninterrupted flow, year after year. Her letters often give an impression of a frenzied activity which was no doubt to blame for the occasional breakdowns in her health, and early death.

Yet in spite of such obstacles, Elizabeth Gaskell was a professional writer. Though she never published anything counter to her principles, much of her work was done for money – to finance a trip abroad for her daughter Meta, to pay for a projected visit to Dresden, or, at the end of her life, to buy a retirement home for herself and William. She wrote on, although 'the very hardest day's bodily work I have ever done has never produced anything like the intense exhaustion I have felt after writing the "best" parts of my books.'

Despite her pioneering approach to subjects that Victorian society largely preferred to ignore, Elizabeth Gaskell's novels were best-sellers during her lifetime. Her first novel, *Mary Barton* (1848), was the earliest literary treatment of England's new northern industrial society by an eye-witness. Before returning to the subject in *North and South* (1855), Mrs Gaskell published *Cranford*, and *Ruth* (1853),

a novel in which – remarkably for its time – the heroine is a prostitute. These were followed by a controversial but highly acclaimed biography, *The Life of Charlotte Brontë* (1857).

Elizabeth Gaskell's later works – *Sylvia's Lovers* (1863), the long story *Cousin Phillis* (1864), and finally, the

unfinished *Wives and Daughters* (1866) – all concentrate on personal relationships. A modern collection, entitled *Mrs Gaskell's Tales of Mystery and Horror*, contains 30 stories whose subjects vary from moral stories to spine-chillers written for the booming Victorian magazine market. Her literary career is the more remarkable for being secondary to her family commitments.

MARY BARTON
◆ 1848 ◆

Jem Wilson loses his young brother (right). Then he loses the love of Mary Barton, a mill-worker's daughter. She rejects him, believing that she has a chance of marrying Henry Carson, the son of her father's employer. Meanwhile, a group of working men, made desperate by poverty and harsh treatment, decide to make an example of the supercilious and unfeeling Carson. Mary's father, John Barton, embittered by his wife's death, shoots Carson, but Jem – known to be Carson's rival in love – is arrested and charged with the murder. When Mary accidentally discovers the truth, it seems that she must choose between incriminating her father or permitting the death of a man whom, as she has realized at last, she really loves.

Subtitled 'A Tale of Manchester Life', Mrs Gaskell's first novel aroused both anger and admiration for its vivid descriptions of working-class misery in the 'Hungry Forties'.

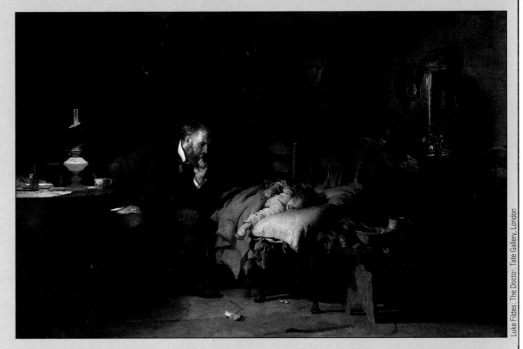

Luke Fildes: The Doctor: Tate Gallery, London

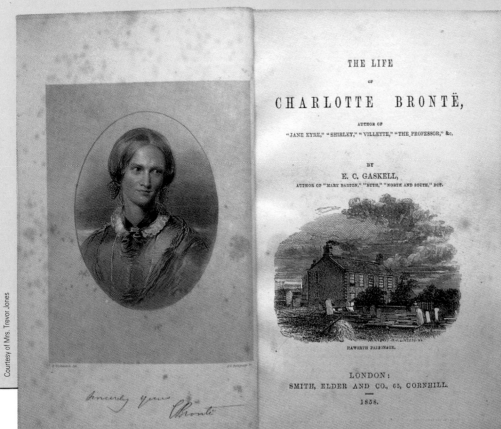

Courtesy of Mrs. Trevor Jones

THE LIFE
OF
CHARLOTTE BRONTË,

AUTHOR OF
"JANE EYRE," "SHIRLEY," "VILLETTE," "THE PROFESSOR," &c.

BY
E. C. GASKELL,
AUTHOR OF "MARY BARTON," "RUTH," "NORTH AND SOUTH," ECT.

HAWORTH PARSONAGE.

LONDON:
SMITH, ELDER AND CO., 65, CORNHILL.
1858.

THE LIFE OF CHARLOTTE BRONTË
◆ 1857 ◆

The subject of Mrs Gaskell's only biography was the famous author of *Jane Eyre*. The two women had been close during the last five years of Charlotte Brontë's life, and Mrs Gaskell had begun to prepare a private memoir of her friend even before Charlotte's father asked her to write a formal biography. On its appearance, *Jane Eyre* had been attacked by one reviewer as the work of a woman who knew too much about passion to be quite respectable, and other critics censured Charlotte Brontë for being obsessed with romance.

Mrs Gaskell was determined to vindicate her memory, and presented her as a lonely, heroic figure and a martyr to duty. She concealed certain aspects of Charlotte's life, notably her attachment to Monsieur Heger, and was forced to make concessions to the sensitivities of the survivors, of whom Mrs Robinson, the presumed cause of Branwell Brontë's downfall, was the most outraged. A third edition of the book was accordingly expurgated. But the original version, now published in full, contains fascinating details and insights, and ranks as one of the biographical classics of English literature.

NORTH AND SOUTH
✦ 1855 ✦

The industrial North of England (right) is contrasted with the rural, leisured South. Margaret Hale is a beautiful, accomplished southerner whose idealistic clergyman father gives up a comfortable living to work as a teacher in a northern cotton town. Though at first repelled by anything to do with 'trade', Margaret comes to sympathize with its badly treated workers. She clashes with John Thornton, a mill-owner who despises her opinions but feels a strong physical attraction towards her.

When Margaret saves him from the angry mob, Thornton misinterprets her motives and proposes marriage. Later he suspects that Margaret is secretly meeting another man, and communicates his suspicion to her. This makes Margaret realize that she loves him. But experience must first teach Thornton a better way of handling his workforce before North and South can be reconciled.

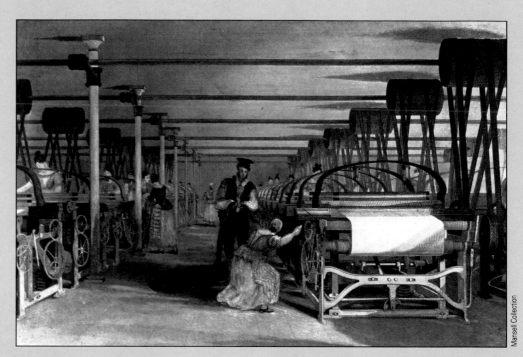

Mansell Collection

TALES OF MYSTERY AND HORROR
✦ 1978 ✦

The Salem Witch trials (below) are the focus of one of the most successful of these tales. *Lois the Witch* is a powerful story of religious hysteria, set in 17th-century New England. Lois, from Old England, finds it hard to adjust to Puritan America, and after a few misinterpreted actions she has to face the most terrible of indictments . . . This modern selection shows Elizabeth Gaskell in an unfamiliar light, as a purveyor of sensational stories, most of them written for Charles Dickens' magazines, *Household Words* and *All the Year Round*. Among the tales in the tradition of the fireside spine-chiller, aimed at the Christmas market, are *The Old Nurse's Story*, in which the unfortunate Miss Furnivall is doomed to re-enact the evil deed of her youth, and *The Ghost in the Garden Room*, in which a worthless son hurts, then haunts, his father and mother. In *The Grey Woman*, a touch in the dark reveals the awful truth about a man to his wife; and an accidental blow leads to an anguished history of concealment in *A Dark Night's Work*. The Victorians had a seemingly insatiable appetite for ghost and mystery stories, and Mrs Gaskell gladly met the demand.

Mansell Collection

SYLVIA'S LOVERS
✦ 1863 ✦

Sylvia Robson (above) is idolized by Philip Hepburn, a hard-working Quaker businessman, but she falls in love with a sailor, Charley Kinraid. Charley is seized by a press-gang, but although Philip knows this, he allows Sylvia to believe that Charley has drowned. When Sylvia's father leads

COUSIN PHILLIS
◆ 1864 ◆

Phillis Holman lives contentedly with her parents on the family farm. Then her cousin, Paul Manning, arrives as part of a team laying a railway in the area. The disruption of country life and tradition by the railways is a major theme of this delightful, nostalgic story.

It is Paul, the narrator of the story, who unwittingly causes much of the trouble that rocks the rural idyll. He introduces Phillis to the head railway engineer, Edward Holdsworth. Although Holdsworth is a 'modern' young man, and Phillis is a country girl, the two are strongly attracted to each other. Holdsworth is offered a post in Canada, and leaves without declaring himself. But he intends to return, and tells Paul – who duly tells Phillis – of his feelings. Phillis is elated, then shattered by the news that Holdsworth has settled in Canada and is engaged to be married. Will she ever recover from the disappointment?

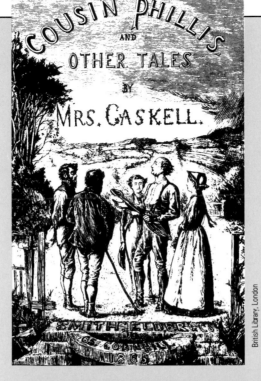

WIVES AND DAUGHTERS
◆ 1866 ◆

Clever, resourceful Molly Gibson and her beautiful stepsister Cynthia (below) are friends, rivals and conspirators in Mrs Gaskell's last, unfinished novel. When the long-widowed Dr Gibson remarries, Molly resents her selfish stepmother, but enjoys the vivacious company of her new stepsister. Molly often stays with the Hamleys, the family of the local squire. They hope to resolve their debts by marrying their elder, favoured son to an heiress – not knowing he is already married. It is the younger son, Roger, who makes good, becoming an eminent scientist. Molly has begun to love Roger, but he is dazzled by Cynthia and they are engaged. Molly helps Cynthia to disentangle herself from a previous attachment, but Cynthia later rejects Roger for a better match. Roger returns from an expedition to Ethiopia, having realized that he loves Molly. Although the text ends at this point, no reader can doubt the fate Mrs Gaskell intended for her characters. Although it is unfinished, *Wives and Daughters* is regarded by some critics as Mrs Gaskell's masterpiece.

an attack on another press-gang, he is hanged, and Sylvia is left destitute. Philip persuades her to marry him, but their life together is joyless and years later, on Charley's unexpected return, Philip flees in shame from their home. Sylvia bears Philip's child, and revelations about Charley diminish her anger at Philip's duplicity. But when Philip reappears, there is no happy ending in store for him.

The Poor Man's Charter

**The appalling poverty that Mrs Gaskell encountered in the slums of
Manchester inspired her early industrial novels – and resulted in
political organization by the working class.**

A bitter choice

*Instead of improving
conditions and pay, British
politicians urged the
starving poor to emigrate,
with promises of impossible
luxury abroad. This 1819
cartoon (below) highlights
this well-fed hypocrisy by
contrasting an image of
violent repression of the
working classes at Peterloo
with a propagandist
depiction of happy people at
the Cape of Good Hope.*

The world of Cranford looks stable and secure at
first sight. In their young days, the Cranford
ladies were those described by Jane Austen,
whirling on the Regency dance-floors of Royal Bath.
But the 40 years which have made Miss Jenkyns "grey,
withered and wrinkled", and Miss Matty too old to
wear an Indian muslin shawl, have also changed the
England in which they live.

When Elizabeth Gaskell published *Mary Barton* in
1848, she wrote to inform the prosperous middle classes of just what was happening in their own country.
Reviewing it, *Fraser's Magazine* wrote, 'People on Tur-
key carpets, with their three meat meals a day, are won-
dering, forsooth, why working men turn Chartists and
Communists. Do they want to know why? Then let

them read *Mary Barton.*' Hers was not an isolated voice.
In that year, newspapers and literature alike were
obsessed with the 'Condition of England' question.
The strains and stresses at work on the fabric of society
were threatening to tear it asunder.

THE PETERLOO MASSACRE

When Elizabeth Stevenson was nine years old, living
with her Aunt Lumb in Knutsford, a crowd of
unemployed weavers and their families – 60,000 of
them – gathered on St Peter's Fields, near Manchester,
to listen to Henry 'Orator' Hunt declaim the cause of
their misfortunes. The police ordered that the speaker
be arrested, but as it was impossible to reach him, the
Hussars were commanded to charge a way through the

defenceless crowd. Eleven people were killed and more than 400 injured. The Government's reputation was destroyed. And the horror of Peterloo lasted long after.

It made a strong impact on the historian Thomas Carlyle, whose writings were, in turn, to influence Mrs Gaskell. He wrote, 'A million of hungry operative men rose all up, came all out into the streets and – stood there. What other could they do? Their wrongs and griefs were bitter, insupportable, their rage against their fate was just.' Peterloo took place in 1819. During the next 30 years, the problems caused by industrial growth, and the grinding poverty of the working man only increased.

BOOMING MANCHESTER

Manchester in the 1830s and 1840s was the pride and the shame of England, the best and worst of places to live. Mrs Gaskell was the friend of many educated and well-intentioned, middle-class Mancunians. But her charity work also took her into poor homes of unimaginable squalor.

The centre of the textile industry, Manchester was making a whole new class rich. Not all achieved their wealth at the expense of their fellow men. Some factory owners organized a shorter (11-hour) day; some ran factory schools for the children working there. The factories themselves were modern, and even critics such as Carlyle acknowledged the thrill of the new:

'Has thou heard with sound ears the awakening of Manchester on Monday morning at half-past five by the clock? The rushing off of its thousand mills, like the boom of an Atlantic tide, ten thousand times ten thousand spools and spindles all set humming there.'

Manchester was at the hub of the new and expanding

James Klugmann Collection

The birthplace of Chartism

Manchester, caught up in the industrial boom of the early 19th century, was a source of great affluence for some – such as the owners of the Bridgewater Canal (right) – but many of its people were homeless and hungry (above). Chartism seemed to be the answer.

City of Manchester Art Galleries

Petitioning Parliament

A huge procession supported the second Chartist petition in 1842 (above); six years later, Feargus O'Connor (right) presented a third petition. Both failed.

railway system. It enjoyed an efficient public supply of gas from 1802, and was manifestly at the forefront of industrial growth.

That same Manchester was, however, the scene of intense suffering for the factory labourers, and of something worse for the unemployed. In the first 40 years of the 19th century, the town had trebled in size. Much of the new housing thrown up was appalling. In 1842 an official report to Parliament compared industrial Manchester with agricultural Rutland: though a labourer's average wages were twice as high in Manchester, the cost of living ate up the extra money and the living conditions in the city were far worse. At a time when an agricultural labourer had a life-expectancy of 38 years, that of a Manchester labourer was just 17. Well over half the children of Manchester labourers died before the age of five. In one area, 380 people shared one privy.

GRINDING POVERTY

In other areas, notably 'Little Ireland', there were no water supplies or sewerage at all, and refuse of all kinds was thrown into unpaved streets built narrow so as to crowd in the maximum number of back-to-back dwellings. Many families had no furniture at all. 'Frequently several families occupied different corners of the same chamber and there was no separation of the sexes, save the distances between beds of straw.'

When the weavers were in work, there was just enough to eat. In the years of slump (which often coincided with bad harvests and a high price for bread) their destitution was complete. Mrs Gaskell recounted to a friend how a father took hold of her arm and, grasping it tightly, said with tears in his eyes, 'Ay, ma'am, but have ye ever seen a child clemmed [starved] to death?' The Rev. R. Parkinson summarized life in Manchester in 1842 saying, 'There is no town in the world where the distance between the rich and the poor is so great, or the barrier between them so difficult to be crossed.'

THE CHARTISTS

The 1832 Reform Act extended the right to vote to most middle-class men. The labouring classes, however, were still without a voice in Parliament. By the 1830s, a feeling was growing that 'the government should do something'. If only working men could be elected to Parliament, surely their grievances would get a fair hearing. Mrs Gaskell's fictional hero, John Barton, expresses their profound anger and sense of injustice: "We're their [the employers'] slaves as long as we can work; we pile up their fortunes with the sweat of our brows, and yet we are to live as separate as if we were in two worlds."

In 1839, the London Working Men's Association drew up the Charter which gave them their name. It attracted support from Manchester, Birmingham and Wales. That year the Charter was presented to the House of Commons by Thomas Attwood, a sympathetic Member of Parliament. The demands were:

'That it might please their Honourable House to take the petition into their most serious consideration, and to use their utmost endeavour to pass a law granting to every man of lawful age, sound mind and uncontaminated by crime, the right to vote by ballot; that the duration of Parliament should in no case be of greater

Kennington Common
On 10 April 1848, a large and angry crowd gathered at Kennington Common, London (below), to support O'Connor when he presented the third Chartist petition. Events like this terrified the propertied classes, who remembered the forced abdication in February 1848 of the King of France, Louis-Philippe (above).

Privileged patriots
The 150,000 'noblemen, gentlemen and other patriots' who rallied to suppress the 1848 rising were lauded by the frightened middle and upper classes. A contemporary song-sheet (right) lionizes these brave defenders of privilege.

PRICE 2/6

Mansell Collection

Guildhall, London/Bridgeman Art Library

Troop trains

The growth of Britain's railway network not only facilitated the movement of goods, but also provided a swift means of transport for special constables. Within hours, they could reach most parts of the country, to quell riots and ensure continued productivity. This was a major factor in the decline of Chartism.

duration than a year; that they would abolish all property qualifications to entitle persons to sit in their Honourable House, and that all Members elected should be paid for their service.' Attwood summed up the needs of the petitioners as 'A fair day's wages for a fair day's work'.

The Charter was greeted with howls of derision by MPs, and the House refused to receive the petition. It was refused again three years later. Meanwhile, bad harvests had forced up the price of bread, a slump threw 10,000 weavers out of work in Manchester alone, and the disastrous Irish potato blight sent thousands of emigrants into the North-West of England.

The revised Poor Law gave out no 'relief' (assistance) except in return for forced labour and the break-up of families. 'Bitter discontent grown fierce and mad' was how Thomas Carlyle described the state of mind of the Chartists.

1848 was a decisive year not only in England but all over Europe. A wave of revolts broke out from the Austro-Hungarian Empire to Paris. And the National Chartist Convention prepared to present its petition for the third time to Parliament.

FEARGUS O'CONNOR

The Chartists had by now just one Member of Parliament – Feargus O'Connor, elected in Nottingham. He was to present the Charter on 10 April. In support of him, a vast crowd of the unemployed, students, strikers, and Chartist sympathizers, estimated at between 15,000 and 100,000 converged on London. This 'Convention' was addressed by speakers who promised to force the Government to accede to their demands. Wild promises of nationalization and redistribution of land struck terror into the property-owners who heard about them. London prepared itself for revolution, with barricades and an army of special constables. One of these special constables was Louis-Napoleon Bonaparte, nephew of the great Napoleon and soon to become the ruler of France.

Palmerston sat in the Foreign Office, his windows blocked with copies of *The Times*. London's defence was put in the hands of the Duke of Wellington. After the Convention, the Duke wrote:

'God knows how many people did attend, but the effect was to place all the inhabitants of the metropolis under alarm, paralysing all trade and business of all description and driving individuals to seek safety by arming themselves for the protection of their lives and those of their neighbours and of their property.'

On the night before, the Chancellor of the Duchy of Lancaster wrote to his brother, 'This may be the last time I write to you before the Republic is established.'

At the last moment, Feargus O'Connor was warned by the Commissioner of Police of the plans to protect London. He faltered then and there. After a long and rambling speech to his supporters, he left the great crowd on Kennington Common and went, with just a small delegation in three cabs, to the House of Commons. The crowd, bewildered, waited for something to happen. Scuffles broke out between enthusiastic special constables and the more zealous of the demonstrators.

Then the rain poured down, and after getting soaked

through, the great Chartist army drifted, cold and wet, to a hundred different refuges. Meanwhile, O'Connor was presenting the Charter, claiming there were 5,000,000 signatures on it. Within a very short time – much too short a time for a proper count to be made, said O'Connor – the petition was declared to have only 1,250,000 signatures, many of them bogus: Queen Victoria and Mr Punch were just two names challenged. The Charter was rejected for the third and last time.

In many cities in the North, rioting and strikes followed, but the action was unco-ordinated and the Chartists' political framework had been shattered. Troop-trains full of special constables were quickly despatched to put down any unrest. The leadership of the Chartists, never outstanding, collapsed. Within a month of his failure, Feargus O'Connor was seen shambling round Covent Garden, his mind broken. Ernest Jones, O'Connor's second-in-command, accused his followers of spending time and money in the 'gin-palace' instead of on the Chartist Movement. In fact grass-roots Chartism survived long after the leadership had withered away.

CHARTISM IN DECLINE

Two changes sealed the fate of the Chartist cause: a slight relief in suffering, combined with the working man's loss of faith that a political Charter would ever improve his life. Trade Unions were beginning to provide a more direct weapon of change. A succession of better harvests brought down the price of bread. The Manchester-based Anti-Corn-Law League organized the import of cheaper corn from abroad in time of bad harvests in England. The Government gradually took

Mansell Collection

No way in
The horror that greeted the presentation of the Charter to the House of Commons is well illustrated by this satirical drawing (above) – as is the despair of the working men promoting it.

A new life
After the failure of the third Charter, many people abandoned hopes of political reform in England. Thousands left to seek a better life in America or Australia (below left).

steps to improve water, sewage and town-planning. And in 1851, Prince Albert's Great Exhibition convinced all but the poorest classes of the advantages of industrialization.

The great downfall of the Chartists lay in their isolation from the middle class. The middle class had organizational ability and some political influence, but the working class, on its own, had none. The middle class did not support Chartism, nor did the successful artisans, and the very poorest members of society were simply unable to sustain a nationwide campaign.

Many of the Chartists found an escape route in the years that followed. At the end of *Mary Barton*, Jem Wilson and Mary turn their backs on the smoke and filth of the cities and emigrate to America. Others left for Australia. In 1848 alone, 250,000 people, most of them from the poorest class, left England for a fresh start. In California, gold was discovered and thousands headed West.

Events in England in 1848 had been influenced by events in Europe. The English upheaval, in its turn, had an impact on Europe. Louis-Napoleon went back to take power in France. Prince von Metternich, who had also taken refuge in London, returned to his former influence in Germany. Karl Marx and Friedrich Engels published the *Communist Manifesto* in 1848 and cited the examples of Manchester factories to encourage German working-class uprisings. It would take some time, however, for those in power to realize that the poor could no longer be ignored.

Ford Madox Brown: The Last of England. Birmingham Museum and Art Gallery

GEORGE ELIOT

→ 1819-1880 →

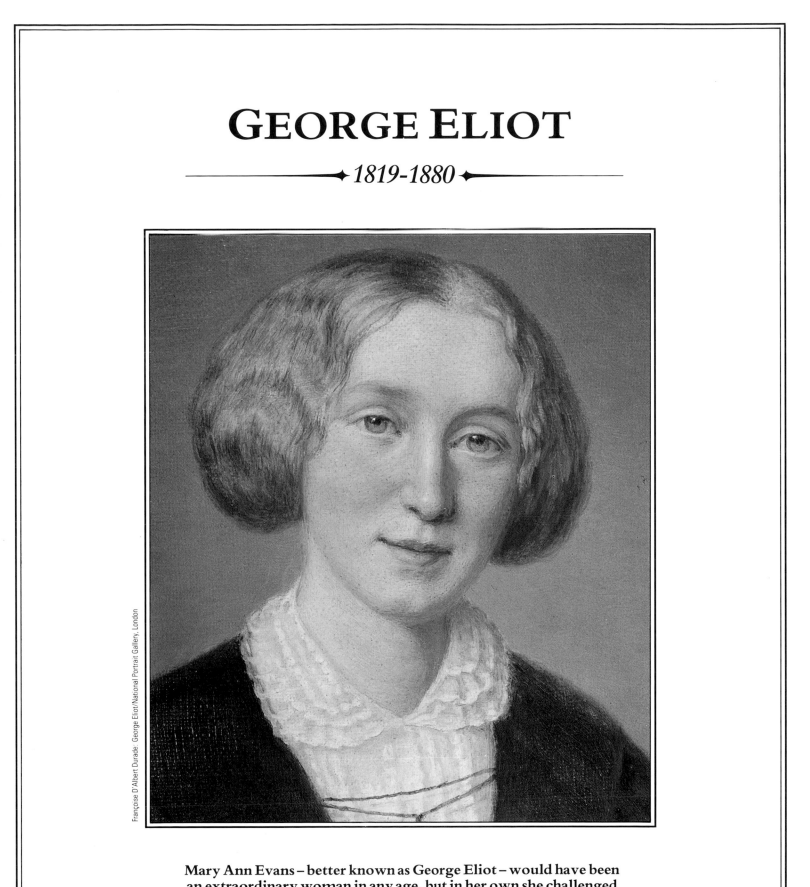

Mary Ann Evans – better known as George Eliot – would have been an extraordinary woman in any age, but in her own she challenged the norms of Victorian social convention and extended the boundaries of fiction. In a period renowned for its strict moral and religious values, she lived openly with a married man and rejected Christianity, but her exceptional qualities as a writer finally gained her – if not complete social acceptance – her rightful position as a great English woman of letters.

The Estranged Intellectual

Mary Ann Evans spent much of her life as a social outcast and wrote her novels under the pseudonym of George Eliot. It was only her formidable gifts that stemmed the relentless tide of public opinion

Ed Buziak

Horace Dudley Studios/Nuneaton Museum and Art Gallery

Warwickshire birthplace
(left) Mary Ann Evans was born in 1819 at South Farm on the Warwickshire estate of Arbury which her father managed for more than 30 years.

Mary Ann's father
(above) Robert Evans – perhaps the inspiration for Adam Bede – was a highly respected practical man. Despite their religious differences, Mary Ann was very close to him.

O f all the million or more words written by Mary Ann Evans, no two were more carefully chosen than those which were to carry her literary reputation: George Eliot – George, she explained later, because it was her 'husband's' name; Eliot because it was easy to pronounce. She carefully chose a male pseudonym to secure for herself 'all the advantages without the disagreeables of reputation'. Yet she divorced herself from many of those advantages, not by her writing but by her choice of a 'husband'. For by daring to live openly with a married man, Mary Ann Evans put herself beyond the pale of Victorian respectability.

Mary Ann was born in Arbury, Warwickshire on 22 November 1819. Her father, Robert Evans, was the estate manager at Arbury Hall, a self-taught man who had started out as a carpenter.

Shortly after Mary Ann's birth, the family, consist-

Coventry background
(right) Mary Ann spent three years at school in Coventry, and lived there for eight years from the age of 21. The town and the countryside around made a deep impression on her and years later, when writing her novels, she was to draw on her memories of the area again and again.
'Middlemarch', the town at the centre of her greatest novel, may be a portrait of the Coventry of her youth – when it was still a quiet, provincial town.

ing of Robert's second wife Christiana and their children Chrissey and Isaac, moved into the comfortable, rambling farmhouse called Griff, which was to be her home for 20 years.

Mary Ann's father and brother were to have an indelible influence on her personality. Her father took her on his inspections of the estate, holding her firmly on the saddle of his large grey horse. Isaac played marbles with her, showed her how to spin humming tops, and took her fishing by the local canal.

At the age of five she was sent to a local boarding school – while Isaac was sent to school in Coventry. The parting from Isaac hurt her deeply, and she hated her time at Miss Lathom's. Four years later, she went on to the Elms School in Nuneaton, where she became firm friends with the governess, Maria Lewis. Under Maria's guidance, Mary Ann became sternly Christian, renouncing her vanity by cutting off her curls and wearing a prim cap. She completed her formal education with a three-year spell at the Misses Franklin's school in Coventry. By the age of 16, she played the piano with refinement, was well read and had completely lost her provincial accent.

A LEARNED 'OWL'

In February 1836, Mary Ann's mother died. When her elder sister Chrissey married the following year, Mary Ann became her father's housekeeper and companion. But she did not neglect her education and took private tuition in German, French, Italian, Greek and Latin, and, in her own words, 'used to go about like an owl, to the great disgust of my brother'. She was rapidly becoming such a formidable paragon of learning that her father feared she would never find husband.

At the age of almost 70, Robert Evans left Griff to Isaac and retired to Coventry where he hoped his 21 year-old daughter would meet potential husbands. Ironically, although he rented a villa in Foleshill, a highly respectable neighbourhood, his choice of house

Mary Ann at 27
(right) One of the earliest known likenesses of the future George Eliot, this sketch was made from a silhouette by Sara Hennell, who also painted the view of Coventry (below left). Sara, Cara Bray's sister, was Mary Ann's best friend for many years, and in her letters Mary Ann often addresses her as cara sposa *('dear wife'). Later she wrote to Sara, 'How many sweet laughs – how much serious pleasure . . . you and I have had together in a past islet of time that remains very sunny in my remembrance'.*

Bird Grove, Foleshill
(right) Robert Evans moved with Mary Ann to this big old house in Coventry in 1841, and it was here she came into contact for the first time with the radical religious ideas that were to become so important to her. Living in the adjoining house were Mr Abijah Pears and his wife Elizabeth, the sister of the freethinker Charles Bray. Charles Bray was an important early influence on the young Mary Ann.

BBC Hulton Picture Library

Mary Evans Picture Library

Horace Dudley Studios/Nuneaton Museum and Art Gallery

Key Dates

1819 born 22 November at Arbury, Warwickshire

1841 to Coventry; meets the Brays

1844 translates a Life of Jesus from German

1849 father dies. Travels in Europe

1854 elopes with Lewes to Germany

1855–78 lives with Lewes

1856 writes fiction

1860 *Mill on the Floss*

1871 *Middlemarch*

1876 moves to Witley

1878 Lewes dies

1880 marries John Cross. Dies 20 December, aged 61

set Mary Ann on the path to social disgrace.

Their next-door neighbour, Mrs Abijah Pears, was the sister of Charles Bray, an enthusiastic social reformer and the most notorious freethinker in Coventry. Mary Ann met him and his wife Cara in November 1841, and they soon became firm friends. Mary Ann had long since believed that it was perfectly possible to be a Christian without being moral, and vice versa; the Brays convinced her that she was right.

On 2 January 1842, Robert Evans' diary notes: 'Went to Trinity Church in the forenoon. . . Mary Ann did not go.' Those two short sentences do not reveal the outrage that shook the family. Robert's daughter had suddenly, she informed him, 'lost her faith in Church doctrine'. And so fierce was his anger that she fled to stay with her sister Chrissey and then Isaac.

Four months passed before her father reluctantly allowed her to return, and Mary Ann agreed to go to church with him. The eruption subsided but the change in her beliefs was irreversible. At the Brays' house she continued to meet influential thinkers such as Robert Owen, the socialist factory owner and, in 1848, Ralph Waldo Emerson, the American philosopher-poet.

In 1844, Cara Bray's brother Charles Hennell gave

Charles Bray

(left) Mary Ann met Charles Bray and his wife Cara soon after she moved to Coventry, and they became life-long friends. Both held advanced views on religion and education, and at their house Mary Ann was able to exchange ideas with such important radical thinkers as Robert Owen and Ralph Waldo Emerson.

George Henry Lewes

(left) Mary Ann and Lewes lived openly together for more than two decades, and they were profoundly happy; on the manuscript to her collected poems she wrote, 'To my beloved Husband, George Henry Lewes, whose cherishing tenderness for 20 years has alone made my work possible to me.' But Lewes was married to another, and Mary Ann became a social outcast.

the trip gave her a lasting taste for travel, and when she reached Geneva she decided to remain there for the winter – staying in a lodging house run by the charming D'Albert Durades. M. D'Albert Durade, a four-foot tall, hump-backed painter, was especially endearing to Mary Ann, and may have provided the inspiration for Philip Wakem in *The Mill on the Floss*.

Mary Ann's future was uncertain. Despite one marriage proposal in 1845, which she had rejected, there were no more likely offers for the 30 year-old spinster. Neither Isaac nor Chrissey wanted a permanent guest in their homes; nor did she relish the prospect. Instead, she took the courageous step of moving to London to lodge at John Chapman's house on the Strand in January 1851.

Chapman, who had just bought the *Westminster Review* (a leading literary paper), took on Mary Ann, now calling herself Marian, as his unpaid assistant editor. She wrote a series of learned articles and, at Chapman's 'open evenings', met numerous influential thinkers including Giuseppe Mazzini, T.H. Huxley, Florence Nightingale, Wilkie Collins, Charles Dickens, Charles Babbage and Herbert Spencer. But her two-year stay in Chapman's house was not easy. Chapman lived there with his wife, two children, and mistress. The two women did not take kindly to another rival and joined forces to drive her out of the Strand for six months from March 1851.

Marian's experience of this unconventional house-

Mary Ann her first writing commission – a translation of a German *Life of Jesus*, which was published two years later by John Chapman in London. And when Bray bought the *Coventry Herald*, she wrote several learned reviews of books on Christianity and philosophy.

To Bray, she was 'the most delightful companion I have ever known; she knew everything. . . But there were two sides; . . . she was frequently very depressed – and often very provoking, as much so as she could be agreeable – and we had violent quarrels'. He also noted her profound need for emotional support, 'always requiring someone to lean on'. In a prophetic analysis of her character made in 1844, the famous phrenologist George Combe noted, 'she was not fitted to stand alone'.

Robert Evans died in May 1849. Mary Ann had nursed him for months, sleeping night after night on the sofa in his bedroom. Now she inherited a modest income of £100 a year – and five days after the funeral left England with the Brays for a journey through France, Italy and Switzerland. Despite her depression,

hold prepared her for the greatest crisis of her life. In 1853, after an unhappy liaison with Herbert Spencer, she fell in love with George Henry Lewes, an actor, novelist, journalist and, later, the author of two highly successful books explaining science to the layman. He was small, lively and so bristling with facial hair that the famous philosopher Thomas Carlyle nicknamed him 'the Ape'.

Lewes' lifestyle was as unconventional as Chapman's. He openly accepted his wife's relationship with their close friend Thornton Hunt and his family. Agnes had had four children by Lewes, and two more by Hunt. Consequently Lewes no longer regarded her as his wife, but having condoned her infidelity, had forfeited the right to sue for divorce.

LONDON OUTRAGE

There could not have been a more unlikely partner for Marian Evans than Lewes. He was as renowned for his sexual laxity as she for her moral probity, yet the attraction between 'the Ape' and the 'great horse-faced blue-stocking' – as Henry James once admiringly called her – was immediate and intense. In October 1853, Marian left Chapman's house for private lodgings; the following July the lovers eloped to Germany, escaping the storm of outrage and condemnation that they had aroused in London. One of their fiercest critics, the sculptor Thomas Woolner – who later became a friend – described them as 'hideous satyrs and

SOCIAL OUTCAST

By living 'in sin' with Lewes, a married man, Marian Evans affronted 'decent' Victorian society. When they eloped abroad, vicious stories circulated back home and, on their return, she was shunned everywhere. Women in particular risked social disgrace if they associated with such a pariah. What hurt Marian most was the hypocrisy. Men could keep mistresses with little embarrassment, but any woman who lived 'in sin' became a social outcast. And adultery was condoned as long as it was kept behind closed doors. It was only because Marian's deeply moral nature would not allow such subterfuge that she was condemned.

Double standards
Victorian society was not as straight-laced as is often portrayed – for men. Men had so much sexual freedom that Dickens once remarked that if his son was not promiscuous he might worry about his health. But for women any hint of sexual scandal was enough to provoke social condemnation.

Christies/Bridgeman Art Library

The shores of Lake Geneva
(left) After her father died in 1849, the Brays took Mary Ann travelling on the Continent – leaving her for five happy months with the D'Albert Durades in Geneva. She fell in love with Monsieur D'Albert as 'father and brother both', and fell in love with travelling too.

Ed Buziak

Arbury Estate
(left) The tranquillity of the Arbury estate where Mary Ann spent her childhood provided the background for much of her earlier fiction, such as Scenes of Clerical Life *(1858) and* Adam Bede *(1859). But the estate was not all peace and quiet; coal had been found on the estate, and production increased throughout Mary Ann's lifetime. In the first tale in* Scenes of Clerical Life, Amos Barton, *she recalls a dismal district of roads 'black with coal-dust' and rows of dark houses 'dingy with smoke.'*

Fact or Fiction

THE ORIGINAL MILL ON THE FLOSS

M any of the settings in George Eliot's novels draw on childhood memories, but the mill on the Floss was an unusual mixture. There is an
element of the old mill at Arbury. But she also had to find a location where
sudden flooding was possible, and detailed research for the book in 1860
reminded her of the tidal surges she had seen on the Trent 15 years earlier.
She combined these memories with close observation of a watermill near
Weymouth to create Dorlcote Mill.

Guildhall, London/Bridgeman Art Library

Realistic idyll
*In Dorlcote Mill, George
Eliot paints an idyllic picture
of an old watermill: "The
rush of the water, and the
booming of the mill, bring a
dreamy deafness, which seems
to heighten the peacefulness of
the scene. And now there is
the thunder of the huge
covered wagon coming home
with sacks of grain . . . and
the unresting wheel sending
out its diamond jets of water."
Yet though the scene is idyllic,
Eliot placed a high value on
realism, and researched her
subject thoroughly.*

Berlin 'honeymoon'
*(right) When Mary Ann
eloped with Lewes in 1854,
they spent three months in
Weimar, which they both
loved, and four in Berlin,
which they found dismal.*

Isaac Evans
*(far right) Stern and pious,
Mary Ann's beloved brother
Isaac cut her off completely
when she lived with Lewes.
Only when she married
Cross did he acknowledge
her again.*

Richmond Hill
*(below) Soon after their
return to London in 1855
Mary Ann and Lewes
moved to Richmond.
Shunned by society, they
had few visitors and often
went walking alone on
Richmond Hill.*

smirking moralists . . . stinkpots of humanity'.

Though the sharpest barbs were launched at Lewes
for deserting his wife, Marian left herself open to attack
as a hypocrite – her translation of Feuerbach's *The
Essence of Christianity* had been published that month,
under her own name. But as she bitterly remarked in
later years, it was her integrity that brought down
society's wrath. If she had secretly become Lewes'
mistress, all would have been well. Victorian society
was more offended by her daring to openly flout its
moral laws – Marian was well aware of the hypocrisy.

In April 1855, Lewes and Marian returned to London and soon moved into lodgings in Richmond. At
first they had few visitors and even fewer invitations.
Her brother Isaac, who still lived in Warwickshire,
was so shocked by their setting up house together that
he disowned her. A further problem was that since
Lewes was still supporting Agnes and their sons, and
her children by Hunt, their finances were limited. But
gradually the barriers lifted. First Chapman, then Bray,
visited Richmond, and Marian began writing again
for the *Westminster Review*.

EARLY FICTION

Without such enforced isolation and with Lewes' encouragement, Marian might never have turned to fiction. Her first three stories – *Scenes of Clerical Life* –
were published under her pseudonym in January 1858.
Her first full-length novel, *Adam Bede*, 'a country story
– full of the breath of cows and the scent of hay', for
which she drew heavily on her childhood memories,
was published the following year. The central character
was based on her father, Robert Evans.

While she was writing *Adam Bede*, her publisher,
John Blackwood, visited Richmond. He guessed that
Marian was the mysterious George Eliot, and agreed
to keep the secret. When the book was published in
February 1859, it attracted tremendous interest and

G.V. Cole, Richmond Hill/Fine Art Photographic Library

Archiv für Kunst und Geschichte

Warwickshire County Library

speculation about the real identity of its author.

Her brother Isaac realized at once that his sister had written *Adam Bede*, but kept it a secret. Other local readers also recognized the characters and background detail, but decided that the real author was a former curate, Joseph Liggins, who had fallen on hard times. To Marian's astonishment, Liggins not only claimed authorship, but also declared that Blackwood had not paid him a penny! This farce turned perilously close to fraud when a group of readers organized a fund-raising committee to compensate Liggins. By mid 1859 Marian was forced to admit her authorship publicly.

The 40 year-old Marian Lewes, as she now called herself, had become famous as the novelist George Eliot. With *Adam Bede's* success – it sold over 5,000 copies in a fortnight – she and Lewes were able to buy a house in Wandsworth.

THE GREAT AUTHOR

The domestic lives of the couple continued almost unchanged for the next 20 years. Marian produced a steady flow of best-sellers from *The Mill on the Floss* to *Daniel Deronda*. The consequent improvement in their financial position (Marian's income rose from £800 for *Adam Bede* to £8,000 for *Middlemarch*) meant that they could afford to take a bigger house, the Priory near Regent's Park, and travel widely in Europe.

But despite her success, she was never entirely socially accepted. Lewes received the invitations, not her. And when people visited the Regent's Park house they often left their wives behind; it tended to be only the more 'emancipated' women who dared the social barbs. But the range of visitors to George Eliot's Sunday afternoons reads like a cultural Who's Who, including Tennyson, Rossetti, Henry James, Edward Burne-Jones and many more.

The success of *Middlemarch* made George Eliot much more socially acceptable as perhaps the country's

greatest living writer. Now a grand dame, she often drove around London in her own carriage, wearing a hat with a giant ostrich feather.

In the mid 1870s, the Leweses began looking for a country house, and enlisted the aid of John Cross, a young stockbroker friend. After two years he found the ideal location – a large red-brick house at Witley in Surrey. But Marian's joy at being back in the countryside was short-lived. Lewes had developed a serious stomach illness, and his health slowly grew worse. By the end of November 1878 he was dead.

For a week, Marian was inconsolable. She remained in her room, and would talk to no-one. Then she began work again, doggedly completing Lewes' final book, then correcting proofs for her own *Impressions of Theophrastus Such*, published in May. Johnny Cross became such a regular visitor that, by the end of the summer, this strangely matched couple, with 20 years difference in their ages, had fallen in love.

They married in 1880 and sailed for a honeymoon to the Continent. While in Milan, they received a letter of congratulation from Isaac, who, for the first time in 23 years, now acknowledged his sister. In December, Mr and Mrs Cross moved into a new home in Cheyne Walk, Chelsea, and began enjoying London life, going to the theatre and concerts. But two weeks later Marian was struck down by a severe kidney infection and after three days of extreme pain collapsed into unconsciousness. She died on 22 December 1880.

The consequences of Marian's social transgression pursued her to the grave – she was denied a funeral at Westminster Abbey as befitted a writer of her undoubted greatness. But her family ties had been fully restored. Isaac Evans was a mourner at her burial, beside Lewes' grave in Highgate Cemetary – so too were many famous men and, significantly, many women, deeply mourning the death of such an inspiring fellow woman.

THE MILL ON THE FLOSS

George Eliot's second and most appealing novel is a moving account of the ties of love, the bonds of duty and the fall and rise of family fortune, taking ordinary lives as the raw material for tragedy.

Completed in 1860, *The Mill on the Floss* was the first novel to reveal George Eliot's enormous talents to the full. Taking as her main theme the 'history of unfashionable families', the author gives a characteristically sensitive, accurate portrayal of 19th-century provincial life – and the story draws on Mary Ann Evans' own childhood for its vivid sense of place, time and domestic tragedy. Its utterly persuasive descriptions of a young girl's loves and hates and fears owe much to this persistent autobiographical detail. And George Eliot's adult experience of being a 'beautiful soul' in a commonplace environment lends the story a convincing sense of real people, in real places undergoing real joys and sorrows.

GUIDE TO THE PLOT

The central family group in the novel is the Tullivers, traditionally provincial people who have lived and worked at Dorlcote Mill on the River Floss for generations. The opening pages introduce the family members and the environment, and also emphasize the relationships between them, providing the reader with a strong sense that they belong to a specific place and time. The opening chapter paints in the surrounding landscape, moving from open fields to the bridge over the River Ripple, tributary to the Floss, then on to the mill and finally to the figure of a small, lively, intense girl, Maggie Tulliver.

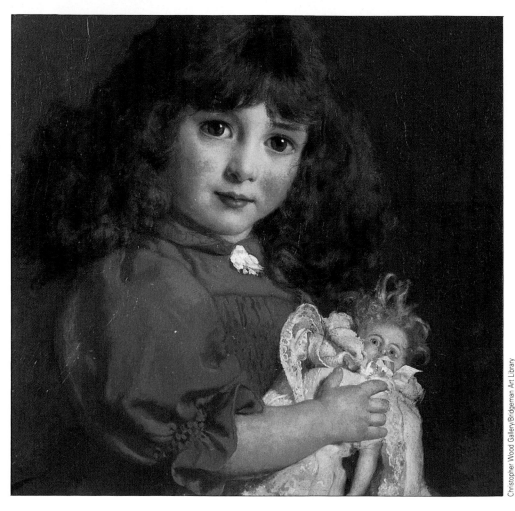

Christopher Wood Gallery/Bridgeman Art Library

> *Surely if we could recall that early bitterness and the dim guesses, the strangely perspectiveless conception of life that gave the bitterness its intensity, we should not pooh pooh the griefs of our children.*

Maggie – bright, quick, raven-haired, dreamy and imaginative – is devoted to her only brother, Tom. Tom is slow in matters of academic work of any kind, shy and awkward in front of aunts and uncles, and unimaginative and dull compared to his younger sister. Yet to Maggie, Tom is an idol and her early life takes its meaning from being in his presence. To the increasingly self-confident Tom, Maggie is someone to control and master when he is not fishing or ferreting with more enjoyable local companions.

The other family of significance is the Dodsons, comprising Mrs Tulliver's three sisters and their husbands. The aunts are staunch representatives of petty bourgeois St. Ogg's society – and its ideas and conventions – and their behaviour provides a humorous undercurrent to the stifling and portentous setting.

Mr Tulliver's persistent use of litigation to protect the flow of water through his mill makes him distrust and hate the local lawyer, Mr Wakem – a hatred that intensifies to the point of obsession. Increasingly stubborn and blinded by hate, he finally loses his land, his property, his self-respect – and his health. He is forced to remove Maggie and Tom from their "eddication", the furniture has to be sold as well as all the "chany" (china) and – final

An eagerness to please
(above) Imaginative and affectionate, young Maggie dotes on her brother Tom and loves to please him, and her spontaneity leads her into "always wishing she had done something different".

degradation in the eyes of the aunts – the linen. And by a supreme irony of circumstance, Mr Tulliver is forced to work as hired manager of his own mill, for the very man whom he sees as his greatest enemy.

The domestic tragedy intensifies when Maggie develops a strong, secret friendship with Philip Wakem, the son of the lawyer, whose interest in the arts matches her own strangely refined sensibility and intelligence.

When Tom Tulliver learns of his sister's secret friendship, he cruelly puts an end to it by threatening to tell their sick father. For

Fine Art Photographic Library

Dorlcote Mill
(left) Maggie and her family live at the mill on the banks of the River Floss, and the opening chapters portray their life as traditional and provincial. The picturesque landscape, and the steady flow of the river, are ever-present elements in the story.

The little gypsy
(below) Mortified by her brother Tom's disapproval, young Maggie impulsively runs away to join a gypsy encampment: she herself is often described as "half wild" and looking like a gypsy. But the gypsies merely return her to her real family.

Bridgeman Art Library

W.D. Sadler: Home Sweet Home (Detail)/Christies/Bridgeman Art Library

The Dodsons
(left) Mrs Tulliver's sisters, the "aunts", and their husbands pay frequent visits to the mill. Their sense of decorum and propriety, and their naked materialism show them to be typical of the petty bourgeois society of St. Ogg's. They frown upon the antics of Tom and Maggie, and compare them in unfavourable terms with their own well-behaved but dull and unimaginative children.

Tom has taken it upon himself to repair the family's honour and restore his father's name by earning money and status in St. Ogg's. This he achieves by natural determination and entrepreneurial flair, but his success in paying back the creditors is followed swiftly by an impetuous act of vengeance on his father's part. Mr Tulliver's long-awaited defiance is his final act – he is too weak to survive it.

Maggie meanwhile grows into an attractive, mature young woman and, returning from a position as governess, she takes up life with her demure, wealthy cousin Lucy. With her she enjoys a spring and summer sojourn that leads with powerful inevitability to a desperate love affair with Lucy's own would-be fiancé, Stephen Guest, the rich, charming and compelling son of an important local banker.

With Philip Wakem back on the scene – still devoted to Maggie – the bonds of love become strangely tangled. Philip arranges for the mill to be returned to the Tullivers at the same time that Maggie becomes embroiled in a web of intrigue and misunderstanding that damages her family still further – always closely scrutinized by the oppressive society

Dishonoured
(left) A stubborn streak in Maggie's father drives him into an expensive lawsuit. When he loses the case to the lawyer, Mr Wakem, he also loses the mill and his self-respect. The Tullivers are forced to sell their cherished belongings – and Tom determines to put things right and restore the family fortunes of the Tullivers.

of St. Ogg's. The last of many reconciliations is with her estranged brother in a powerful scene that brings the family saga to a tragic conclusion.

A 'NATURAL HISTORY'

The Mill on the Floss does not fall easily into a specific category of fiction. However, along with her other early novels, George Eliot called it 'a natural history' in which she presents 'history incarnate' (embodied in a person or persons). By natural history – and by placing people in environments – George Eliot allows the action to unfold and avoids the restrictions of a fictional plot.

The most successful and ultimately memorable element of the book is the writer's characterizations, particularly of Maggie herself. And her character is revealed against a closely defined background of a specific corner of England and placed in a specific society. Both are painted with unerring accuracy. The social background, the strong sense of family ties, the stifling materialism of the society of St. Ogg's, and the underlying theme of the repression of women within this society and the role of women as arbiters of good taste and social values – all heavily influence the way in which the characters act, but George Eliot always gives their actions a personal motive and a realistic reason. The novel takes the reader along with it at a natural pace rather than by manipulation of a plot.

> *... one more touch, one more glance might be snatched. For, why not? ... they had confessed their love, and they had renounced each other – they were going to part. Honour and conscience were going to divide them.*

Similarly, the town of St. Ogg's is presented as ' history incarnate'. It is referred to as "a continuation and outgrowth of nature . . . which carries the traces of its long growth and history like a millenial tree . . . It is a town 'familiar with forgotten years'".

The most striking theme in the novel is that of the effects of family ties. The relationship between Maggie and Tom is one that has a major bearing on the way Maggie's character and actions unfold. The ties within the family are fundamental to our understanding of the action and to the way in which the society is structured. George Eliot sets up this relationship and the family background with a pen that defines every angle vividly.

Common to both families is the sense of kinship, and it is a sense that perverts as well as enriches the lives of both. The aunts all regard Mr Tulliver as a hot-tempered man, they think of Maggie as peculiar because of her gypsy-like complexion and wildness, but they stand by the family dutifully – because sister Bessy is a Dodson.

The Dodsons were a proud race, and their pride lay in the utter frustration of all desire to tax them with a breach of traditional duty or propriety. A wholesome pride in many respects, since it identified honour with perfect integrity, thoroughness of work, and faithfulness to admitted rules: . . . To live respected and have the proper bearers at your funeral, was an achievement of the ends of existence that would be entirely nullified if, on the reading of your Will, you sank in the opinion of your fellow men, either by turning out to be poorer than they expected, or by leaving your money in a capricious manner, without strict regard to degrees

THE CHANGING FACE OF COMMERCE

Mr Tulliver's preoccupation with fending off the aggressive activities of other mill owners depicts new industrial methods challenging, and destroying, the old. The peace and tranquillity of long-established traditions at Dorlcote Mill are sharply contrasted with the zealous banking, investment and commercial activities of St. Ogg's. Mr Wakem the lawyer personifies this new capitalism, and Tom Tulliver quickly learns to turn it to advantage. Though the society of St. Ogg's regards such entrepreneurship as admirable, the novel questions the ethics of a system that turns people like the Tullivers into its victims.

St. Ogg's is a historic town which is dramatically changed by the "incongruous new-fashioned smartness" of commerce.

of kin. The right thing must always be done towards kindred.

In such a way George Eliot depicts the Dodsons. Theirs is a creed that stands in a very poor light when genuine need crops up – as it does when Mr Tulliver loses his mill and his fortune. At this stroke, the Dodsons are eager to demonstrate their support by buying the family linen from "poor Bessy" as well as some of the china and other goods. Helping in any more fundamental way is outside the bounds or understanding of their strict, mutually defined family code. It is interesting to note, however, that the strictest and most critical of the aunts, Mrs Glegg, is the one who, "doing right by her kin", offers to take in Maggie Tulliver when the rest of the society of St. Ogg's are happily villifying the young woman for an action that represents a breach in their homespun etiquette.

"THE LITTLE WENCH"

It is within this strong family bonding and sense of duty that Maggie and Tom's actions are made poignant and ultimately tragic. Maggie will not act against her brother's strongly held obligations to their father in regaining the family honour and the possession of the mill – even if it means having nothing to do with Philip Wakem. She is fully aware of the futility of the feud and the effect it has on her own possible happiness with Philip, but the family comes first. Through the bonds of kinship Maggie, largely self-taught but never reaching the full potential of her 'higher nature', never grows to full self-knowledge. Her filial nature has a repressive rather than uplifting quality, leading her to extreme self-sacrifice and a distorted sense of her obligations to her family. The skill and beauty of the book, however, has a great deal to do with the way George Eliot makes the reader empathize with all the twists and turns of Maggie's thinking.

A secondary theme in the book is the way in which women in general and Maggie in particular are by far the second-class citizens. Maggie is much brighter than Tom, her mind is quicker, her understanding and sensitivity is more fully developed at an early age. But she is always "the little wench" in her father's eyes, even on his deathbed, and takes second place to Tom in her education and in her degree of importance in the Dodson family's opinion. George Eliot does not register her own indignation at this treatment but, as with the rest of the book, demonstrates Maggie's subordination merely by unfolding in vivid detail the quality of Dodson and Tulliver social life. Later in the book, in the scenes at Lucy Deane's house, Maggie suffers as the women behave in a manner that becomes the ladies of gentility. "Only those who have known what hardest inward conflict is can know what Maggie felt as she sat in her loneliness . . . only those who have known what it is to dread their own selfish desires as the watching mother would dread the sleeping-potion that was to still her own pain". George Eliot's success is that she made her readers feel as Maggie did.

Higher ideals
(left) Maggie's love for Mr Wakem's son, Philip, awakens her passion for the arts, but alienates her from her brother.

Reconciliation
(below) Tom's rigid sense of honour and Maggie's love for Philip inevitably separate them, until tragedy finally reunites them.

C.E. Perugini: Idle Moments/Fine Art Photographic Library

CHARACTERS IN FOCUS

George Eliot's major achievement in *The Mill on the Floss* is her rendering of characters who are realistic and compelling, set against a backcloth of everyday provincial life. Maggie Tulliver is the central and most complex figure, but her irascible father, her dominating brother, her placid and fearful mother – all play their part in the family tragedy. And outside the family relationships, the author's eye for detail is no less painstaking and astute.

WHO'S WHO

Maggie Tulliver Extremely imaginative and affectionate, Maggie dotes on her brother and father. Her family regard her as "comical" and subordinate to Tom, and she grows up with a "keen sense of unmerited reproach".

Tom Tulliver Maggie's dominating older brother. His overwhelming desire is to achieve mastery over others, which he calls "justice". His rigid sense of right and wrong makes him a determined businessman.

Mr Tulliver Head of the "proud" family, owner of the mill and "hot-tempered", he fears change and distrusts lawyers.

Mrs Tulliver The "good-tempered" and placid mother, who was once good-looking but not "o'er cute".

The "aunts" Mrs Tulliver's sisters who represent petty bourgeois St. Ogg's. Mrs Pullet, a hypochondriac in permanent fear of dying. Mrs Glegg, a noisy, interfering busybody. Mrs Deane, the snobbish wife of a proud self-made man.

Philip Wakem A bright and sensitive young man, isolated from society by his deformity, who falls in love with Maggie. But his lawyer father is the cause of the Tulliver's downfall.

Stephen Guest Handsome and charming friend to Philip Wakem and fiancé to Maggie's cousin Lucy Deane. He typifies male sexual magnetism.

The "aunts" are typical of the oppressive and small-minded society of St. Ogg's: "surely the most prosaic form of human life: proud respectability in a gig of unfashionable build". They are entirely obsessed with material worth.

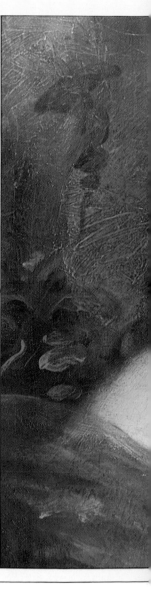

"saucy, defiant Stephen" Guest (above) has "an air of nonchalant leisure" and is engaged to the beautiful Lucy. But he compromises Maggie with his attentions to her.

Philip Wakem is "a pale, puny fellow" made lonely and intense by his physical deformity. Given to bouts of peevish oversensitivity, he proves to have great virtue and an undying adoration for Maggie.

Maggie (below) *is "a creature full of eager, passionate longings* . . . with a blind, unconscious yearning for something that would…give her soul a home…" Her growth to adulthood shows a refined sensitivity held in check by her family and society. Her thirst for knowledge gains her a companion in Philip Wakem, but her love for him is never fully distinguished from pity or from the simple desire to be loved. Her love for Stephen Guest is based on a sexual attraction for which she is woefully ill-equipped.

Victoria and Albert Museum/Fotomas

"Mr Tulliver was on the whole a man of safe traditional opinions." Though he dotes on his daughter, he is "hot-tempered" and distrustful of the world outside Dorlcote Mill – especially lawyers. In his stubborn battle against lawyer Wakem, he loses his mill and his self-respect and eventually his life. Of Maggie, his "little wench", he proudly boasts that "she'd ha' been a match for the lawyers, she would" but he is anxious only to have his son well educated.

In young Tom Tulliver (right) it is "impossible to discern anything but the generic character of boyhood" – except a rather stubborn streak. At the age of 13, "he would punish everybody who deserved it: why, he wouldn't have minded being punished himself if he deserved it, but then, he never did deserve it".

Fine Art Photographic Library

ENGAGING SYMPATHIES

**George Eliot's genius lay in her rare ability to make her readers
feel what it is like to be someone else. Her aim was to promote
people's compassion – and she succeeded magnificently.**

While writing *The Mill on the Floss*, in 1859, George Eliot stated the principle that informs the best of her fictional work. 'If art does not enlarge men's sympathies, it does nothing morally . . . The only effect I ardently long to produce by my writings is that those who read them should be better able to *feel* the pains and joys of those who differ from themselves.'

The belief that people can be improved through the twin experiences of suffering and joy, whether in real life or through reading about them, is the backbone of George Eliot's fiction. It is the central theme of her seven great novels, in each of which the principal characters grow in moral stature through their 'clear-eyed endurance' of pain. The doctrine replaced her religious beliefs, which she abandoned in her early twenties.

In the early novels – *Scenes of Clerical Life*, *Adam Bede* and *The Mill on the Floss* – Eliot partly captures our interest and sympathy by reinforcing her characters and locations with her own detailed observations of real life. In fact, on one occasion she even portrayed an elderly cleric so accurately that she had to apologize to him for intruding into his privacy.

In her masterpiece, *Middlemarch*, George Eliot draws on experiences from her time in Coventry. The period was now sufficiently distant to be viewed confidently and with detachment, bearing out her earlier remark that 'my mind works with the most freedom and the keenest sense of poetry out of my remotest past'.

SPIRITED HEROINE

Middlemarch reworks the way in which George Eliot's own freethinking Coventry neighbours, the Brays, released her 'chained' intellect. The spirited heroine Dorothea's disastrous marriage to the dry and scholarly Casaubon gives way to an idyllic love for Will Ladislaw – a relationship which frees Dorothea's personality and intellectual powers. The love story is embedded in a portrait of England in the mid-19th century that is unsurpassed in literature for its detailed observation of a living, changing society.

George Eliot further manages to engage our sympathy by letting us see her characters develop into the people they are. Her characters are very social – and socially evolving – people. Her four major heroines – Maggie Tulliver, Dorothea Brooke, Romola and Gwendolen Harleth – all begin as egoists who gradually mature as they come to recognize that others have an "equivalent centre of self".

The Mill on the Floss was George Eliot's first novel written according to this precept. The central characters, Maggie Tulliver and her brother Tom, are based on her own childhood self and her brother Isaac. Their closeness and subsequent alienation reflect the way in which her real-life brother refused to acknowledge her when she started living with George Henry Lewes. Similarly, Tom is hurt when Maggie innocently spends the night with Stephen Guest – he feels that Maggie

Ed Buziak

Country memories
George Eliot's early works are firmly rooted in the Warwickshire countryside of her childhood. Many fictional places and characters have real-life originals. Arbury Hall (left), where her father (himself a model for Adam Bede) was estate manager, is Cheverel Manor in Scenes of Clerical Life.

Social beings
(right) Eliot gives her characters a definite social context, and they develop their "inward being" partly from their relations with others – in their family and the wider community. Most of her novels draw upon her knowledge and experience of provincial society in mid-Victorian England.

Ordinary people
*Eliot admired the
everyday realism and
'truthfulness' of Dutch
paintings such as* The
Kitchenmaid *by Jan
Vermeer (right). In her
writing, she focused on
the personal dramas
experienced by ordinary
people, and she thought
that artists should give
'loving pains' to the
'faithful representing of
commonplace things'
rather than concern
themselves with grand,
ideal themes.*

J. Vermeer: The Kitchenmaid/Rijksmuseum, Amsterdam

British Library

Manuscript of a masterpiece
(left) Middlemarch *begins with a description of
Dorothea – "Miss Brooke". The novel began as
two separate stories; one entitled* Miss Brooke,
*the other concerning Dr Lydgate. Eliot recognized
the parallels between them – both main characters
had their ideals defeated by misguided marriages –
and wove them together to form her masterpiece.*

Christies/Bridgeman Art Library

has disgraced herself, him and their family
name irredeemably.

George Eliot herself described the heroine
of *Middlemarch*, Dorothea, as emerging out
of "moral stupidity", having regarded the
"world as an udder to feed her supreme self".
By the end of the novel, she is almost being
compared to a saint, whose "unhistoric acts"
add to "the growing good of the world".

Eliot's later novels were shaped by her profound sense of the psychological and social
laws that govern human conduct. Each deci-
sion, each character's action – however trivial
– is directed by psychological and social laws.
It is a view that can be seen in *The Mill on
the Floss*, if only in its embryonic stage. There
are no easy solutions – "one course seemed
as difficult as another" to Maggie Tulliver.
And Maggie, like George Eliot, is forced to
endure "inward suffering that is the worst
form of Nemesis".

LINKS WITH THE PAST

The idea of Nemesis – the inescapable consequences of one's past – is a central one in
Eliot's work. It finds one of its most powerfully poetic expressions in the tragic figure of
Mrs Transome in *Felix Holt*, who carries the
painful secret that her beloved son Harold is
the result of an illicit affair with her lawyer
Jermyn. When Harold, an aspiring politician,
threatens to expose Jermyn's infamous dealings with the Transome estate, he does not
know that he is threatening his own father,
his mother – and himself. He asks his mother
why she persists in shielding Jermyn, but she
cannot tell him:

*Mrs Transome's rising temper was turned in to
a horrible sensation, as painful as a sudden concus-
sion from something hard and immovable when
we have struck out our fist, intending to hit something warm, soft and breathing, like ourselves.
Poor Mrs Transome's strokes were sent jarring
back on her by a hard unalterable past.*

The imagery is shocking in its originality
and raw physical intensity. And by using the
words "we", "our" and "ourselves" rather
than "she", "her" and "herself", Eliot encourages the reader to feel *with* "poor Mrs Transome", as well as for her.

Although Eliot had consistent fictional
aims, she realized them in different ways as
her writing developed and matured. *Silas
Marner*, published in 1861, signalled a change
of approach from her first two novels, *Adam
Bede* and *The Mill on the Floss*. It was the first
to be set outside the Midlands, and was not
based on herself or on any other real people.
And the story of a miserly recluse reclaimed
by the love of a child received more poetic
and symbolic treatment than her early works.
She completed the novel in less than five
months and received enthusiastic reviews.

But far greater changes were underway.

When *Silas Marner* was published, George Eliot was in Italy with Lewes, conducting extensive research into the events and personalities of medieval Florence for *Romola*. She continued researching on their return to England, rather against Lewes' view that this was too scholarly an approach.

EXPERIMENT AND RESEARCH

She followed this with another experiment, *The Spanish Gypsy* (her poetic drama), and then *Felix Holt*, which also required much background research. But in 1871 Eliot returned to her previous source material, the familiar scenes of her later youth. The return – aided by her mature thinking, her confirmed beliefs and the application of 'natural history' to human development – led her to write one of the greatest masterpieces of the English language, *Middlemarch*.

Eliot herself was well aware of the increasing force of her ideas, and acknowledged the difficulty of moulding them on to realistic characters and making them 'thoroughly incarnate, as if they had revealed themselves first in the flesh and not in the spirit'.

PUBLISHED SUCCESS

Meanwhile, Lewes was also experimenting. As her business manager he was able to tempt rival publishers who wanted to handle a potentially profitable author. George Smith bought the copyright for *Romola* for the huge sum then of £7,000 but found that he had bought a novel that sold disappointingly in both serialized and volume form. The author, however, was not too dismayed. *Romola* received some good reviews and was profitable.

George Eliot's earlier novels had been published in three volumes, usually priced at 31/6d per set (and selling to libraries) and then in a single volume for 12/-. But *Middlemarch* appeared in eight half-volumes, priced 2 guineas. This scheme, suggested by Lewes, brought in more than £8,000, and was also used for her last novel, *Daniel Deronda*, which was even more successful.

Eliot's most pugnacious advocate, the critic F. R. Leavis, argued that her greatness lies in her unflinching portrayal of the causes and effects of human suffering, and her insistence on dealing with the realities of life. She shows how sympathy and love can emerge even in the most hostile circumstances.

Consequently, some interpret the manner in which Eliot engages her readers' sympathy for her leading characters – who come through difficult circumstances as better, wiser people – as being a subconscious plea for an understanding of her own plight. Her fiction can also be read as a distinguished – and successful – attempt to regain her rightful place in the social world.

Inspired by Liszt

(above) Eliot's impression of the genius and charisma of the great pianist Liszt – 'His face was simply grand – the lips compressed and the head thrown a little backward' – whom she met in 1854 may have inspired the character of Klesmer in *Daniel Deronda*.

The final heroine

(right) In *Daniel Deronda, the beautiful, strong-willed heroine Gwendolen Harleth meets her future husband Grandcourt at an archery match where she is enjoying the general admiration of her "grace and power". She expects to retain such power in her marriage, but Grandcourt's "strongest wish is to be completely master of this creature". For many, the profound and tragic psychological portrait of Gwendolen is Eliot's greatest achievement.*

George Eliot turned to fiction writing late in life; she was almost 40 when her first novel *Adam Bede*, an overnight success, was published in 1859. Until then, she was best known for her reviews. She confirmed her reputation with *The Mill on the Floss* in 1860, and gained financial security with *Silas Marner*, which appeared the following year.

During an experimental phase, she abandoned the portraits of English country life that she had made the subject matter of her early fictions, setting *Romola* (1863) in 15th-century Italy. But the mainstream of her work concerns the fates of individuals bound up in English society. *Felix Holt* (1866) and her mature master-piece *Middlemarch* (1871-2) are both set in 'Loamshire' – the fictional Warwickshire – in the 1830s.

Many critics comment upon the difference between the pastoral charm of Eliot's first three novels and the philosophical weight of her last three. But by the time of her last novel *Daniel Deronda* (1874-6) George Eliot was recognized as the greatest English novelist of her age.

ADAM BEDE

→ 1859 ←

Hetty Sorrel (left), with her kitten-like beauty and inability to resist temptation, is at the centre of Eliot's first full-length novel. She is loved by the honest carpenter Adam Bede, but seduced by the young squire Arthur Donnithorne. 'A country story, full of the breath of cows and the scent of hay', it is darkened by Hetty's threatened execution for the murder of her own baby.

The story was inspired by the real-life experience of George Eliot's aunt Elizabeth Evans, who appears in the novel as the Methodist preacher Dinah Morris. She had once spent the night in the condemned cell at Nottingham Jail, comforting a prisoner through the final hours leading to her execution for infanticide. The novel was greatly admired for its realism and detailed scenes of Warwickshire life. A world-wide success almost overnight, it had *The Times* describing George Eliot as 'among the masters of the art' of the novel.

ROMOLA

→ 1863 ←

Fifteenth-century Florence (above) – when the religious zealot named Savonarola seized power from the ruling Medici family – is the setting for *Romola*. Savonarola governed the city briefly before being overthrown and burned at the stake. His career provides the framework for this historical romance.

Romola, the virtuous and devoted daughter of an old blind scholar, is a supporter of Savonarola, but her faith turns to disillusionment as he becomes embroiled in various political intrigues. At the same time she turns against her opportunist husband, the cynical Tito Melema and leaves the city to administer to the sick.

The novel required massive research, and many readers have found it heavy-going. But others have praised the imaginative descriptions of the Renaissance city, and the penetrating portraits of historical characters.

E.H. Courbould: Hetty Sorel and Captain Donnithorne in Miss Poyer's Dairy(detail) Reproduced by gracious permission of Her Majesty the Queen, Royal Library Windsor

Scala

MIDDLEMARCH
✦ 1871-72 ✦

The elderly Reverend Casaubon (left) and young Dorothea Brooke (below) lead us into the world of *Middlemarch*. The novel brilliantly intertwines a number of major and minor plots, the most important of which involves the fate of Dorothea.

The young, naïve and idealistic heroine is "enamoured of intensity and greatness, and rash in embracing whatever seemed to her to have those aspects". She finds her aims thwarted by the narrow restrictions of provincial life and yearns to pursue some large, noble cause which she imagines is represented by the scholarly Casaubon. But she realizes as early as their disastrous honeymoon that they are hopelessly mismatched, and that what she convinced herself was her husband's intellectual greatness is mere pedantry.

Dorothea befriends the lively and generous Will Ladislaw, Casaubon's younger cousin. But Casaubon is so suspicious of his wife's growing intimacy that he states in his will that if she ever marries Ladislaw she will forfeit her inheritance.

Other plots involve the mayor's children, Fred and Rosamond Vincy. Fred is torn by his obligation to his father to become a clergyman, and the refusal of his love, Mary, to marry him unless he renounces the Church and pursues a career of his own. Meanwhile, Rosamond pursues the eligible Dr Lydgate, but their marriage and his idealistic aspirations are undermined by her thoughtlessness and materialism. Lydgate's eventual downfall is linked to that of Middlemarch's hypocritical banker, Bulstrode.

The principal characters are set against a detailed portrait of Victorian provincial and urban life, and the political struggles between the Tories and Reformers. What makes the novel particularly impressive is the manner in which Eliot dramatically shows how human aspirations and vocations can be sabotaged by unforeseen events, which are themselves the result of an accumulation of countless minor decisions and motives which have created unavoidable, relentless forces.

Middlemarch is far more than a love story involving Dorothea Brooke. It is one of the greatest novels in the English language and has been praised as a 'treasure-house of detail' by Henry James, and by Virginia Woolf as being 'one of the few English novels written for grown-up people'.

Christies/Bridgeman Art Library

Fine Art Photographic Library

Manchester City Art Galleries

FELIX HOLT
✦ 1866 ✦

Workers (above) provide the social focus of Eliot's 'political' novel, *Felix Holt, the Radical*. It is set in 'Loamshire' in the early 1830s, when Harold Transome returns home after 15 years to take over the family estate, following the death of his elder brother.

Although Harold comes from a powerful Tory family, he is standing as a Radical candidate. But Eliot pointedly contrasts his politics with the idealistic Radicalism of Felix Holt. Transome's electioneering is the antithesis of Felix's humanitarian attempts to rouse the local workers to believe in their rights and self-worth.

The heroine of the novel is Esther Lyon, who is forced to chose between Harold and Felix, between wealth and compromise or poverty and principles, and between destructive and creative political forces. When Felix is tried for murder following a riot, Esther determines to give up the sterile luxury of Transome Court for him.

Eliot thoroughly researched the political issues involved in the novel but, for most readers, the political element is not as successful as the more private and more moving dramas experienced by Harold's mother, Mrs Transome.

The real imaginative greatness of *Felix Holt* springs mainly from this tragic portrait of an ageing woman for whom "the great story of this world" is "reduced . . . to the little tale of her own existence". Mrs Transome's life is a "living death" dominated by the guilty secret about her son's real father and her fear that Harold will discover the truth. While Harold concerns himself with politics, she lives, ignored, in "silken bondage" and "well-cushioned despair".

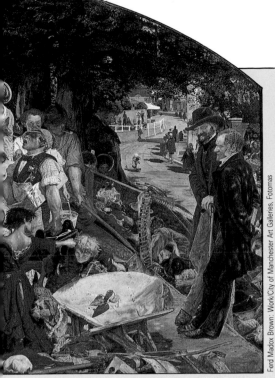

Ford Madox Brown: Work/City of Manchester Art Galleries, Fotomas

SILAS MARNER

◆ 1861 ◆

Eppie, (below) a tiny golden-haired orphan, limps into Silas Marner's cottage one New Year's Eve, and the embittered old miser believes his stolen treasure has been returned in human form. His love for her gives the weaver a new life.

Not surprisingly, a book which ends on such a happy note – "O father," said Eppie, "What a pretty home ours is! I think nobody could be happier than we are." – has been dismissed as a fairy tale. But for George Eliot it was more a 'legendary tale, suggested by my recollections of having once, in early childhood, seen a linen weaver with a bag on his back'.

Silas Marner is one of Eliot's most popular novels, widely admired for its good humour, and for scenes such as that at the Rainbow Inn, with the butcher and the farrier quarrelling fiercely over red Durham cows and the parish ghost.

J.C. Horsley: The Contrast: Age and Youth/Victoria and Albert Museum/Bridgeman Art Library

Christies/Bridgeman Art Library

DANIEL DERONDA

◆ 1876 ◆

Gwendolen Harleth is losing at gambling (above) at a fashionable European resort, when she is first seen by Daniel Deronda. Later, when Gwendolen suffers an even greater "gambling loss" in her marriage to the wealthy, but sadistic Henleigh Grandcourt, it is on Deronda that she becomes dependent for spiritual support. It is assumed that Deronda is Grandcourt's illegitimate cousin, but it transpires that he is the son of a renowned Jewish singer. On discovering his true origins, Deronda becomes increasingly drawn to Mirah, a young Jewish singer. When Grandcourt dies in a boating accident which Gwendolen feels she could have prevented, she again turns to Deronda. But he has decided to marry Mirah and devote himself to the Jewish cause. Critics have disparaged the novel's Jewish elements, but the portrait of the vain, egoistic Gwendolen growing to self-knowledge through suffering is one of Eliot's triumphs.

Questioning the Faith

The spiritual crisis experienced by George Eliot was symptomatic of the Victorian age, and – paradoxically – provided much of the intellectual and emotional energy of her novels.

E.H. Courtbold: Dinah Morris preaching on Hayslope Green/Reproduced by gracious permission of Her Majesty the Queen, Royal Library, Windsor

For most educated Victorians, religion lay at the very centre of life. The people who believed were in deadly earnest – but so were those who, like George Eliot, doubted or denied the supernatural, and worked out their own purely secular creed. The age was one in which sects and parties multiplied within the churches, while, almost simultaneously, new ideas and scientific advances undermined the very foundations of religion. For all their energy and self-confidence, the Victorians were oppressed by doubts, and George Eliot herself experienced an acute religious conflict difficult to imagine today.

During the 18th century, the Christian churches in England lost a good deal of their vitality. The Church of England, in particular, became as much a social institution as a religious organization, teaching its parishioners to chant,

> *Bless the squire and his relations*
> *And keep us in our proper stations.*

Many families were like the Dodsons and Tullivers in *The Mill on the Floss* – "they didn't know there was any other religion, except that of chapel-goers, which appeared to run in families, like asthma". And the clergy resembled their vicar, who "was not a controversialist, but a good hand at whist, and one who had a joke always ready for a blooming female parishioner".

The Evangelical movement developed as a reaction to this state of affairs. It was not a new sect, but a powerful general impulse that was felt within almost all the Protestant churches, and was essentially a revival of Protestant values. Evangelicalism stressed the importance of the individual's experience of conversion and replaced the Church's authority with a personal interpretation of the Scriptures. The movement was responsible for the creation of one new breakaway sect – the Methodists, followers of the Anglican clergyman John Wesley, whose willingness to preach in the fields or market-place angered his superiors. As a result, Methodism reached many thousands of working men and women in the great new industrial towns, who were virtually ignored by the Church of England.

However, the Evangelical wing of the Anglican Church was also active – and influential – in changing social conditions. Its ranks included such outstanding figures as the anti-slavery campaigner William Wilber-

Wolverhampton Art Gallery/Bridgeman Art Library

Christies/Bridgeman Art Library

A materialistic clergy
(above) During the 19th century clergymen were becoming increasingly conscious of social status, like Mr Stelling in The Mill on the Floss, *who "had a true British determination to push his way in the world".*

The persuasive Methodist
(left) Women as well as men taught the doctrines of Methodism, following the example of John Wesley, who preached in the open to working people. George Eliot's aunt was one such preacher, the model for Dinah Morris in Adam Bede.

force, and Lord Shaftesbury, who was responsible for the earliest legislation regulating hours and conditions of work in Britain's factories.

The Evangelicals were devotees of preaching and lectures, and poured much energy into philanthropic societies, and raising money for foreign missions. They dressed soberly, observed the sanctity of the Sabbath and tended at the slightest provocation to proclaim their allegiance in the universal battle between sin and salvation. At best, the Evangelical was heroic; at worst, pompous, sanctimonious or even hypocritical, like Mr Bulstrode in George Eliot's *Middlemarch*, who had "an immense need of being something important and predominating".

THE OXFORD MOVEMENT

George Eliot knew Evangelicalism from the inside. Under the influence of her teacher, Miss Maria Lewis, she held strict Evangelical beliefs until she was 22. She refused to go to such a sinful place as the theatre with her brother Isaac (although she later regretted the impulse to deny him 'what I now see to have been quite lawful amusements'), and her first publication was a religious poem in Evangelical vein.

Evangelicalism remained the dominant religious 'style' for most of George Eliot's lifetime, although a substantial minority of Anglicans, including her brother Isaac, were drawn in the diametrically opposite direction – towards the Tractarian or Oxford movement led by the High Church intellectual, John Henry Newman who was to exert such an influence over the young Oscar Wilde. Newman and his followers reasserted the importance of ritual and the sacraments, rejected the individualism of the Evangelical tradition and made the Church rather than conscience the basis of theological authority and the means of salvation. They even went so far as to argue that the Church of England was not Protestant at all, but a purified form of the Catholic Church and should have no truck with Protestant 'heretics'.

The publication of the 'Tracts for the Times', which set out the movement's principles, caused a furore almost inconceivable today. Hostility towards Roman Catholicism was still widespread, and to most Protestant Englishmen the doctrines of the Oxford movement seemed bent on 'Romanizing' the Church of England. Such fears were strengthened by defections to Rome, the most sensational being that of Newman himself, who later became a Cardinal.

Pomp and circumstance
(left) At one extreme of the fermenting religious controversy lay High Anglicanism, which made full use of ritual and its trappings. Buildings and services alike were lavish and splendid, indicating the wealth invested in this branch of the Church.

Looking towards Rome
(right) The most influential man behind the Church's movement towards Rome was the Oxford vicar, John Henry Newman. He persuaded as much by his personal devoutness as by his powerful writings. But his later conversion added fuel to the widespread Protestant hostility to the Catholic 'threat'.

National Portrait Gallery, London

Sources and Inspiration

In the early 19th century, those in authority had no doubt that the function of religion was to uphold the social order, and that atheists and deists (people who believed in God but dispensed with all dogma and ecclesiastical authority) were likely to be dangerous revolutionaries. One such was the poet Shelley (also a radical, a vegetarian, and an apostle of free love), who was sent down from University College, Oxford, in 1811 for his pamphlet 'The Necessity of Atheism', the first advocacy of complete unbelief to be published in English. Later, Shelley was beaten up at Keswick, probably because of his religious opinions.

Attempts to convert the working class to atheism and radicalism were continued by agitators like George Holyoake, the last man in England to be imprisoned for professing atheism. However, secularist propaganda touched only a small section of the working class, although working people long remained vaguely anti-clerical because of the presumed alliance between the Churches and the propertied class.

This assumption was weakened by the rise of a socially concerned group, the Christian Socialists, in the middle of the century, but neither they nor the 'slum parsons' and energetic church-builders of the late Victorian period managed to reverse the trend towards mass irreligion. Its sympton was the decline in church- and chapel-going, and it signified indifference rather than any positive commitment to secular beliefs.

By contrast, writers, scientists and intellectuals experienced serious religious crises and conflicts throughout the Victorian period. If their numbers were not great, their influence was widely felt, and George Eliot's circle included many men who had refused to take holy orders or abandoned them as a matter of conscience. For some, loss of faith was experienced as a liberation from the gloom of Original Sin and the threat of hell-fire. George Eliot herself cast off Evangelical Christianity with a 'feeling of exultation and strong hope', her soul 'liberated from the wretched giant's bed of dogmas on which it has been racked and stretched ever since it began to think'.

Others, like Thomas Carlyle, were overwhelmed by the meaninglessness of a universe without God, although 'From suicide a certain aftershine . . . of

Walker Art Gallery/Bridgeman Art Library

The Romantic atheist
(above) One of the earliest advocates of atheism was the Romantic poet Percy Bysshe Shelley, whose radical views clashed alarmingly with the English establishment, and drove him to settle in Italy. Shelley's dramatic life ended prematurely when he drowned in a summer squall at sea. His body was burned on the shore, in keeping with ancient Greek custom and his own unorthodox views.

Herbert Spencer
(below left) One of the great Victorian liberal philosophers, Spencer elevated science into a religion, and was a vigorous advocate of Darwin's theory of evolution. His progressive views were of great interest to George Eliot and gave intellectual stimulus to their friendship.

Slavery and the Church
(right) An Evangelical convert, William Wilberforce, was among the first to denounce the evils of the slave trade, and to campaign against it. The Emancipation Act – which abolished slavery in Britain and its colonies – was finally passed in 1834.

Christianity withheld me.' The note of doubt and melancholy is strong in Victorian literature. It was given its classic expression in Matthew Arnold's poem 'Dover Beach', where only the 'melancholy, long, withdrawing roar' of the Sea of Faith is heard.

BROKEN FAMILY TIES

As well as private agonies, the Victorian doubter had to endure the disruption of personal relationships. Religious differences broke friendships and – even more important in a family-centred age – divided parents and children, brothers and sisters. George Eliot's experiences in this respect had many parallels. When she refused to go to church, her father moved away and their differences were only patched up when she agreed to conform outwardly. Her Methodist uncle Sam, less easily placated by conventional gestures, broke off all contact with her. And religious differences created a distance between George Eliot and her beloved brother Isaac, although it was her liaison with George Henry Lewes that occasioned the final break. As late as 1869 she noted sadly that 'I cling strongly to kith and kin, even though they reject *me*.'

The chief cause of this turmoil was the impact of science, particularly on the credibility of the Bible. Every advance in knowledge broadened the picture of a universe governed by general laws and working through the logic of cause and effect. The area in which miracles might plausibly occur grew continually smaller, whereas the 'miracles' of technology – that is, applied science – multiplied. More specifically, the Higher Criticism, which was mainly a product of German universities, applied scholarly method and rules of historical evidence to sacred texts, and drew devastating conclusions as to their truth and reliability. George Eliot was profoundly influenced by this sort of Biblical criticism, and translated into English David Friedrich Strauss's *Das Leben Jesu*, which stripped the life of Christ of all its supernatural elements.

Victorian orthodoxy sustained one shock after another, but the severest came from what George Eliot called 'The Doctrine of Development': the concept of evolution, which undermined belief in a single Creation and in fixed moral standards – and much

Evangelical practice
(above) Evangelicalism was responsible for the founding of numerous religious societies and foreign missions, and to this end was indefatigable in its fund-raising activities.

Transforming society
(below) The appalling working conditions in Britain's mines and factories were seen as a matter of Christian – as well as political – concern by certain leading church figures. The most notable was Lord Shaftesbury, who had the power to effect radical social changes.

else. George Eliot's friend Herbert Spencer applied the concept of evolution to human society. Charles Darwin's *Origin of Species* substituted biological evolution for a single act of creation which left species forever fixed. The process of natural selection – 'the survival of the fittest' – was also at variance with the idea of a benevolent creation. Instead, as the poet Tennyson lamented, there was 'Nature, red in tooth and claw'.

THE DESCENT OF MAN

Darwin's book appeared in November 1859, while George Eliot was working on *The Mill on the Floss*. Though judging it 'ill-written', she recognized at once that 'it makes an epoch', and she and Lewes became convinced Darwinians. Darwin himself was anxious to avoid trouble, and omitted almost all mention of the most controversial issue – human development – from *Origin of Species*. But orthodox critics were quick to realize that natural selection implied the descent of man from some ape-like creature – an intolerable insult to a being 'created in God's image', and an implicit subversion of the moral framework of existence. Denounced by many, Darwin's theories found an able defender in the brilliant scientist T.H. Huxley, who tirelessly publicized and debated them. In the course of one such debate at Oxford, the glib Bishop Samuel ('Soapy Sam') Wilberforce enquired on which side of his family Huxley claimed to be descended from an ape. Darwinism survived and ultimately forced the churches to rethink and restate their orthodoxies.

Avowed atheists also achieved public acceptance, although many preferred to call themselves 'agnostic'. This term was coined by Huxley, and he thereby discreetly stressed his lack of certain knowledge con-

cerning the existence of God, rather than his disbelief. By 1888, after an epic series of elections and ejections, Charles Bradlaugh had established the atheist's right to become an MP, and to give evidence in a court of law, without swearing by a deity he believed to be non-existent. Nonetheless, in 1878, a British court decided that Bradlaugh's colleague Annie Besant, who had published *The Gospel of Atheism* the year before, was not a fit person to have custody of her daughter.

In reality, the Victorian atheist was a morally earnest person. George Eliot was therefore in many respects a representative figure, like the philosophers who influenced her. She translated Ludwig Feuerbach's *Essence of Christianity*, which argued that the splendid qualities, hitherto projected on to God, must be found among the mutual relationships of humans. And she admired the Positivism of Auguste Comte for its would-be scientific approach to society and its 'religion of humanity', though she was evidently well aware of its slightly absurd side.

Neither Feuerbach nor Comte was crude enough to denounce Christianity. Their view of it as a necessary phase in human development appealed to George Eliot's strong feeling for the past and the old ways, expressed in the gallery of sympathetic portraits of clergymen and pious folk that occur in her works. For George Eliot herself, unbelief was no easy option. In a now famous passage, F.W.H. Myers has recorded how she, 'taking as her text the three words which have been used so often as the inspiring trumpet-calls of men, – the words *God, Immortality, Duty* – , pronounced, with terrible earnestness, how inconceivable was the *first*, how unbelievable the *second*, and yet how peremptory and absolute the *third*.'

A shocking theory (above) In 1859, the naturalist Charles Darwin published his monumental work, Origin of Species, and rocked the very foundations of Church and society. To the theory that species survive and develop by a process of natural selection, Darwin brought a body of scientific evidence based on his researches in South America, the South Seas and the Antipodes. The ensuing row between science and religion reached a peak in a famous debate at Oxford between Bishop Samuel Wilberforce and the biologist T. H. Huxley (above left). On this occasion science emerged triumphant, and Huxley continued to be the most tireless champion and exponent of Darwin's theory, saying in 1881 that if the idea of evolution had not existed, they 'would have had to invent it'.

BIBLIOGRAPHY

Ashton, Rosemary, *George Eliot.* Oxford University Press (New York, 1983)

Auster, Henry, *Local Habitations: Regionalism in the Early Novels of George Eliot.* Harvard University Press (Cambridge, 1970)

Beer, Gillian, *George Eliot.* Indiana University Press (Bloomington, 1986)

Bentley, Phyllis, *The Brontës.* Thames & Hudson (New York, 1986)

Blom, Margaret, *Charlotte Brontë.* G. K. Hall (Boston, 1977)

Briggs, Asa, *Iron Bridge to Crystal Palace: Impact and Images of the Industrial Revolution.* Thames & Hudson (New York, 1979)

Brodetsky, Tessa, *Elizabeth Gaskell.* St Martin's Press (New York, 1986)

Chase, Karen, *Eros and Psyche: The Representation of Personality in Charlotte Brontë, Charles Dickens and George Eliot.* Methuen (New York, 1984)

Cross, J. W., *George Eliot's Life as Related in Her Letters and Journals* (reprint of 1885 edition). Richard West (Philadelphia, 1973)

Davey, Cyril, *John Wesley and the Methodists.* Abingdon Press (Nashville, 1986)

Dewes, Simon, *Marian: The Life of George Eliot.* Haskell (Brooklyn, 1974)

Duthie, Enid L., *The Brontës and Nature.* St Martin's Press (New York, 1986)

Epstein, James, *The Lion of Freedom: Feargus O'Connor and the Chartist Movement, 1832-1842.* Methuen (New York, 1982)

Gerin, Winifred, *Emily Brontë.* Oxford University Press (New York, 1972)

Goldring, Maude, *Charlotte Brontë, The Woman* (reprint of 1915 edition). Folcroft (Folcroft, 1976)

Haldane, Elizabeth, *George Eliot and Her Times.* Haskell (Brooklyn, 1974)

Hale, Will T., *Anne Brontë: Her Life and Writings* (reprint of 1929 edition). Arden Library (Darby, 1978)

Harrison, G. E., *Haworth Parsonage: Study of Wesley and the Brontës.* Folcroft (Folcroft, 1937)

Jones, David, *Chartism and the Chartists.* St Martin's Press (New York, 1975)

Lansbury, Coral, *Elizabeth Gaskell.* G. K. Hall (Boston, 1984)

Law, Alice, *Patrick Branwell Brontë* (reprint of 1923 edition). Folcroft (Folcroft, 1976)

Messinger, Gary S., *Manchester in the Victorian Age: The Half-Known City.* Longwood (Wolfeboro, 1985)

Moore, Virginia, *The Life and Eager Death of Emily Brontë* (reprint of 1936 edition). Haskell (Brooklyn, 1971)

Nestor, Pauline, ed., *Female Friendship and Communities: Charlotte Brontë, George Eliot, Elizabeth Gaskell.* Oxford Universtity Press (New York, 1986)

Peters, Margot, *Unquiet Soul: A Biography of Charlotte Brontë.* Atheneum (New York, 1986)

Pike, Royston, E., ed., *Human Documents of the Industrial Revolution in Britain.* Allen & Unwin (Winchester, 1966)

Pollard, Arthur, *Mrs Gaskell: Novelist and Biographer.* Harvard University Press (Cambridge, 1965)

Sadoff, Dianne P., *Monsters of Affection: Dickens, Eliot and Brontë on Fatherhood.* Johns Hopkins University Press (Baltimore, 1982)

Shuttleworth, Sally, *George Eliot and Nineteenth-Century Science.* Cambridge University Press (New York, 1987)

Stoneman, Pasty, *Elizabeth Gaskell.* Indiana University Press (Bloomington, 1987)

Swinnerton, Emily, *George Eliot, Her Early Home.* Folcroft (Folcroft, 1974)

Tjoa, Hock G., *George Henry Lewes: A Victorian Mind.* Harvard University Press (Cambridge, 1977)

Tuttle, Robert G., Jr., *John Wesley: His Life and Theology.* Zondervon (Grand Rapids, 1982)

Whitehill, Jane, *Letters to Mrs Gaskell and Charles Eliot Norton.* Folcroft (Folcroft, 1932)

Whitfield, A. Stanton, *Mrs Gaskell: Her Life and Work.* Folcroft (Folcroft, 1929)

Wilkes, Brian, ed., *The Illustrated Brontës of Haworth: Scenes and Characters from the Novels of the Brontë Sisters.* Facts on File (New York, 1986)

Wilson, Romer, *The Life and Private History of Emily Brontë* (reprint of 1928 edition). Haskell (Brooklyn, 1972)

Wright, William, *The Brontës in Ireland.* Portals Press (Tuscaloosa, 1985)

INDEX